full moon
LUNARANTICS

dark exploits in the lake district

By John McCarthy

Published by JJMoffs Independent Book Publisher 2021

A CIP catalogue record for this book is available from the British Library.

JJMoffs Independent Book Publisher Ltd
Grove House Farm, Grovewood Road,
Misterton, Nottinghamshire DN10 4EF

ISBN 978-1-8383697-6-7

Typeset and cover design by Anna Richards   www.design-by-anna.co.uk

DESIGN BY ANNA

For Wendy, Kate and Jack.

My amazing adventurous family.

about this book...

This book has been much discussed by those whose monthly full moon adventures feature in it. It aspires to be more than a logbook, an almanac of our Howlings; it aims to inspire and enthuse others into deeply exploring their own local environment at night. We have discovered that even places we know well like Blencathra or Ullswater, look and feel so different in the dark. We have been blessed to see them bathed in glorious moonlight, when we are the only ones there to embrace the new found world of Lunarantics. We have also seen them obscured by rain, cloud, hail and snow but let's not let the truth get in the way of a good story... Equally importantly, we have howled in some amazing places that were previously unknown to us, on land and water, above and below ground. Even for those of us who know The Lakes well, it has been an odyssey of discovery, a labour of love, an ongoing dark adventure.

The book is also a huge testament to friendship. The poet Edgar Guest wrote in his 1915 poem "Faith" "That strangers are friends that we someday may meet", in the 1960s the Irish Tourist Board misattributed the often used misquote "There are no strangers here, only friends who have not yet met" to their famous son W.B. Yeats and it has appeared on posters and T shirts ever since... This hackneyed adage has never been truer than when applied to the Howling Folk. From the earliest conversations with Dom, James and Dave and the subsequent launch email, our aspiration was to actively search out and attract like-minded people who we didn't previously know, to join us on our nocturnal meanderings. This has proved to be the real success story of the influence of the Full Moon. Of the regular Howlers who, like planets, orbit around the monthly gatherings, over half of them were completely unknown to me when I sat around our dining room table with those three close friends in early July 2012 and said "I have this idea I have been chewing over for a while, please bear with me...".

To understand the concept, it might help to know a little of my background... so, please bear with me...

about the author...

Life is a journey is a well-worn saying. Mine has been an adventurous journey so far, full of long rambling stories that eventually get to the point... Eventually...

I regard myself as a fairly normal chap; born on the outskirts of an ever-growing London conurbation but only a short bus or train ride away from the extensive Surrey countryside and the North Downs. Other folk might find me slightly eccentric, but I hasten to disagree... I am who I want to be - me.

Life was fairly straightforward during the 70s and most of the 80s; school, Cubs, Scouts, friends, family camping holidays, exams, Saturday job and eventually full time employment. Then in 1986 something changed, I often reflect upon one particular day when I was nineteen, when I was called into an appraisal meeting with my Director. He suggested that I was proving to be an asset and they would like me to undertake additional training and develop my role, with additional benefits including a company car and a very attractive company mortgage scheme. Well, that freaked me out completely, I had an epiphany; it was only a job, I was clearly working far too hard, taking it too seriously, I was young

and needed to live my life, not sell out to "the man", not at nineteen! So, having said yes to the attractive pay rise and commenced a training programme, I saved as much money as possible until in January 1987 I left work and to the surprise of many, I became a traveller, a backpacker, a citizen of the world, moving slowly around the globe in a vague Easterly direction, starting in Egypt and eventually flying home from New York twelve months later. Life was challenging and full of choices every day. Adventures beckoned, misadventures happened, life was eaten in large chunks and sometimes the world spat me out again, but often it smiled on me, introducing me to wonderful people and amazing places... It was truly

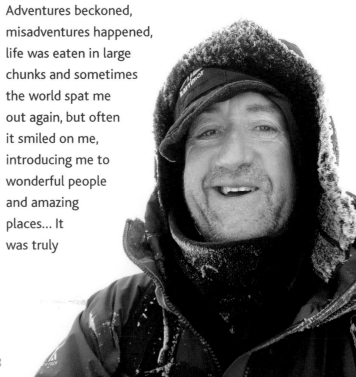

transformational. Physically and mentally I matured, no challenge was too much for me, until I ran out of money and came home in need of employment. That period of transition was a challenge and within three months I had saved up enough money to head to Europe with a tent for another summer of daily choices and random chaos. I was alive and loving it....

Until inevitably I ran out of cash again and landed back in the UK in Winter. Then life took a turn and what started off as a temporary Christmas job in my local record shop ended up as a five year career managing some of the largest record shops in London. Money flowed as did the beer, numerous gigs and music industry parties were attended. I bought myself an MG BGT and a Wurlitzer Juke Box. My language became endowed with song lyrics and mystical messages from the likes of Dylan, Young, Crosby, Fairport, Sandy Denny, Christy Moore, The Pogues and The Levellers. Holidays and long weekends were times for adventures, to head to The Brecons, The Peak, The Lakes, to camp, to explore, to generally arse around in the outdoors with friends. These escapes from London provided me with the freedom of the road; choices and decisions were my own again and work was left behind.

Then I had an epiphany - I was clearly due another. I would love to tell you it was a message from Jim Morrison or brought on by the early death of Freddie Mercury. But my influences were changing, this was the mountains talking to me. One glorious Autumn day in 1992 whilst sitting in The Chair near the summit of Red Pike, looking at Wasdale and The Scafell range I realised that I didn't want to go back to London. I wanted to escape, to live in The Lakes and have adventures and fun, what a great life that would be...

So, I hatched a plan. Obviously I needed to give up work again, buy a maroon 1974 V4 Ford Transit campervan, bum around for eighteen months gaining experience and some hard won outdoor qualifications and convince my long suffering girlfriend Wendy to move to The Lakes where I would get a job as an outdoor instructor. So, that's what I did. It hasn't always been easy but it has been a lot of fun; Wendy and I got married, our house grew with a growing family as Kate and Jack arrived and I enjoyed many adventures at work and with our extended family.

One of the constants in my life is that along the way, I have had the pleasure of making friends with some of the most amazing people. Some of them are rogues, scoundrels, adventurers, beer drinkers and hell raisers, others are much more considered and philosophical. As an introverted extrovert I love them all.

When you work in outdoor learning, many of your colleagues are highly accomplished mountaineers, kayakers, rock climbers, cavers etc. I am more of a generalist, a competent outdoor professional who has had years of pleasure designing and delivering powerful outdoor learning and development programmes for people of all ages and backgrounds, from the classroom to the boardroom. Family adventures were increasingly exciting, we travelled to a wide breadth of other National Parks and our family adventures in The Lakes were duplicated and enlarged upon on an international scale in Europe and North America - the adventures got bigger and better! But somewhere in the back of my mind something was lacking... At the age of 45 was I actually considering having a mid-life crisis?

The MG BGT had long since rusted away into the great scrapyard in the sky. The Wurlitzer misplayed more often than not, my Scarpa Vegas and technical axes were not getting as much use as they had... Was it time to buy a motorbike, dust off my motor bike licence which I had paid that friendly Indonesian policeman two USD for in 1987, squeeze into my David Crosby-esque fringed leather jacket and hit the road like Hopper, Fonda and Nicholson... or was there a less radical option...?

Forever running around my brain were mystical lyrics from the past, including;

Neil Young advising me that "It's hard to teach a dinosaur a new trick, lately I've been finding out I'm set in my ways", Neil certainly made me ponder on my creativity.

Pink Floyd's reflections on growing old have always resonated deeply with me "The memories of a man in his old age are the deeds of a man in his prime". Was I past my prime already, looking backwards more than forwards? Surely there was still a road to travel.

The Boss has his own thoughts on the perils of ageing "Glory days, well they pass you by... in the wink of a young girl's eye " Was Bruce encouraging me to relive my own Glory Days, they had provided me with no shortage of great memories and associated stories.

And from Uncle Neil's seminal Rust Never Sleeps Album, Mr Young reflects that "How I lost my friends I still don't understand". That is a worrying thought indeed, only made slightly more accessible when you consider some of the friends he is probably talking about...What was it that Roger, Bruce, Old Neil and others were trying to tell me...? The message was there surely, if only I could decipher it... Another epiphany was looming, it was actually overdue.

What I clearly needed, what I have always needed was more uncertainty, more adventure, more mishaps, more stories of high challenge and fun. The sort of adventures I had when I was young - full of like-minded friends causing chaos and howling with laughter.

The message was there all along, I had just been playing the wrong songs, listening to the wrong albums! I needed Van the Man, Bowie, Soft Machine, The Doors, The Waterboys, The Cowboy Junkies, Fairport Convention and of course my constant companion Old Neil... I needed a "Moondance", a "Moonage Daydream", to see the "Moon in June", to take a "Moonlight Drive", to wonder at "The Whole of The Moon", to understand the "Blue Moon" cycle, to witness "The Rising of the Moon" on a monthly basis, to howl at the "Harvest Moon" with Neil. I needed it all. It had been there all along in so many songs, pieces of art, movies and TV programmes. I needed to get out more, clearly alongside Ozzy Osbourne to "Bark at the Moon". If only Frank Sinatra was still here to "Fly Me to the Moon", so I could get "Drunk on the Moon" with Tom Waits... Now that would be a Full Moon

Adventure. I clearly needed to gather a group of like-minded folk and head out into The Lakes on a moonlit journey of discovery.

Please join me to hear more about our Lunarantics...

first thoughts on lunarantics

The initial concept was undoubtedly influenced by a variety of previous lunar experiences.

I have always been aware of the Moon. It is after all our nearest celestial object and appears regularly in the sky, often during the day which can be confusing until you understand what it is up to. Along with Dog, Cat and Sun, Moon must be one of the earliest words we learn to speak, read, and write. The Moon is justifiably popular in nursery rhymes, what with cows jumping over it and a man living in it... It is clearly a major part of our lives and for many of us it has an attraction all of its own.

In my early years of adventuring, a night hike with Cubs and Scouts was often a highlight of camps as the dark added a different dimension and it was easier to attack each other. In teenage years we often staggered up to a small white roundabout behind the locked gates of Richmond Park and sat on "The Moon" to relax with friends. During my wider adventures in the UK with my old buddies Matt and Rob, we were often exhausted by our daylight exploits and the night was mainly for sleeping or walking back from the pub... This all changed when visits to The Alps introduced a new phrase to my vocabulary,

now an infamous phrase in my family: An Alpine Start. For those unfamiliar with the concept, it involves planning to get up and start your mountaineering day several hours before sunrise to make the most of a safe ascent on hard snow before the sun heats the face, and ice and rock may then fall on those late out of bed. In these circumstances, the light of the moon can prove very useful.

This was confirmed on an early trip to The Alps. Some friends and I were staying at the Cosmiques Hut above Chamonix. As part of our acclimatisation we had an unplanned snooze in the hut and then thought that an afternoon ascent of the Cosmiques Arete was in order. Queues of folk with their Guides at the cruxes slowed us down a lot and we eventually summited after dark. Much to our delight the descent back to the hut from the Aiguille Du Midi cable car station was soon floodlit by a highly luminescent Full Moon bathing our route in an absolutely stunning light and amazingly, we had The Alps to ourselves.

Some years later a friend, Steve, who eventually became a regular Howler, and I were trying to align our diaries for some winter climbing on Helvellyn. Work and family life clashed with weather conditions and so my solution, remembering the Alpine Moon, was to climb at night. Once again we were rewarded with perfect conditions as a big digestive biscuit of a moon rose above The Pennines just as we were on the head wall and it cast our shadows onto the snowpack in front of us. We were exhilarated by the experience and could not believe our luck; great conditions, great company, a Full Moon and the whole mountain to ourselves... There was definitely a theme developing.

The importance of the light and the guidance supplied by the Moon was reinforced when one of my oldest friends, Matt and I met to have a canoe expedition on the River Severn. True to form we had a long lunch stop, followed by an early evening refreshment stop and it was getting dark before we focused on locating a canoe bivi site. Unfortunately, the riverbanks then became very steep with no obvious egress for about five miles and we found ourselves paddling in the dark. There was no moon. It got very dark and this heightened our other senses. Particularly our

hearing; small shingle rapids started to sound like Niagara Falls and in the days before LED headtorches, visibility was poor and our speed and reactions may have been slower than usual due to the day's lengthy refreshment stops. We eventually found a muddy cattle trod down to the river, dragged the canoe up into a field, pulled a tarp over the top of it and set up camp, adding this story to a long list of the other adventures we had had together over the previous 25 years. I missed the moon on that great trip, but at least I realised it and thus an idea was forming....

lunar mission planning

At the age of 45 life for me living on the edge of The Lake District National Park was good: Family✓ House✓ Career✓ Friends✓

International Holidays✓ own canoe rack full of a variety of boats✓ Maslow would be proud of me, my basic needs were well met, or were they? Where was the sense of belonging, the big adventures that defined my youth? We were having lots of great family fun; fell walking, canoeing, wild swimming, camping, and often other friends joined us with their families as well. However, I still yearned for a bit more, the unknown, the thrill of adventure and exploration. Slowly, the idea of a monthly nocturnal gathering of like-minded adults began to form... but we couldn't meet at weekends because that was family time, and Wednesday was canoe club and Thursday was parent taxi, and I was often away with work one or two nights a week... how was this ever going to work? Then the Moon inspired me, some quick research showed me that the Full Moon fell on different days each month, so as long as we planned ahead and accepted that not everyone would be able to attend every month we were in business.

But who would join me for these Lunarantics?

the usual suspects

That was clearly the obvious answer, the usual suspects. Work had provided me with a fine group of friends, my extended family; we met frequently, we worked on each other's house projects, we celebrated birthdays together, we had a wide array of outdoor skills and associated toys, we drank beer and danced together. Of course Dom, James and Dave would want to get involved in some extra-curricular Lunarantics. Hence the July 2012 dinner table conversation to float the idea which then led to an email to confirm our thoughts and launch the idea of Full Moon Gatherings.

The original email eventually got circulated to a wider friendship group to drum up broader support. I still have a copy of it today. It says:

"We are all busy people; we all have family and work commitments.
We would all benefit socially, physically and mentally from having some more adventure and fun in our lives. Hence the suggestion for Full Moon Fever (Thank you Tom Petty).
We should try and commit to one evening a month, the night of the Full Moon where a group of like-minded friends get together just for the craic.

I am keen to involve more people than just us four and to extend the group outside of current or ex-colleagues, so we get a different perspective.
Members of the group should be fit and able and likeminded to avoid unnecessary conflict of opinion.
Due to summer holiday commitments and lead in time, I suggest the first gathering should be on Sunday 30th September.
I fully appreciate that not everyone will be able to attend all Full Moon Fever evenings, hence the need for a larger pool.
No fixed venue, no fixed format, no fixed timings or agenda. All suggestions open to consideration and debate.
Could you all consider two people whom you might like to invite to get involved. Probably living in the North West, although guests, visiting friends etc should always be welcome.
We should also consider how we involve our families.
Let's open up an email conversation and see what you think.
We might even enjoy it! I am off to practise my howl."
John 17.7.2012

the first howl; oh, what a night, late september in 2012

Various discussions in between summer holidays had helped us to realise that we were actually on to something. The idea would float. Other people were genuinely intrigued, interested even. Before we had even had a night out together, our friends Paul and Steve1 had decided they would like to get involved in the proposed Lunarantics.

We knew that we needed a great story to tell other folk about the sort of adventures we were aspiring to. We had to start with a bang, not a whimper. We needed an adventure full of heroic exploits, with a dash of derring-do. The sort of thing Errol Flynn would get up to on a break from filming Robin Hood or The Sea Hawk. We had to be daring - we needed an exploit we could be proud of, something to get some wind under the sails of this Full Moon thing, something with rakish elan. Something we did not normally do, had never done before...

So, we decided to invade Scotland. Not by land though, that is just a quick drive up the M6, we would invade across The Solway, Viking style.
What could possibly go wrong?

Well, that was a great question. We needed success, not failure. We needed to ignite a fire under ourselves and others, and we certainly needed to avoid a damp squib at all costs. So, we planned; we claimed to be outdoor professionals after all. We studied maps and charts, we reviewed the weather and the tide, we discussed personal and group kit. Did we really need a first aid kit, or would we just bring the wounded home? We thought we had thought of everything, that we were ready. If only we knew...

Come the glorious 30th September only three of the six of us invited could actually attend - me, Dom and Dave. We chose our means of transport; Dave and I would paddle over in a double ocean kayak, Dom would go full Errol Flynn and sail his topper. Oh, what fun we would have, we laughed. Little did we know that the Gods were laughing also...

This story has been recounted so many times now, you may even have already heard it, more than once probably! It has become a touchpoint, a beacon of what we still strive to achieve. As with many other subsequent Full Moon nights

out, it has been discussed so much, it has taken on a life of its own - a thing of beauty and legend, to be cherished, by me anyway.

The detailed plan was to cross the Solway, landing in Scotland to the East of Annan. We were to launch from east of Glasson at high tide and then use the outgoing tide to take us back to England, landing to the west of Bowness on Solway where we had a second vehicle to shuttle boats and bodies back to the start.

Here are some excerpts from the Full Moon report that we circulated to all, after that first eventful evening:

full moon fever #1

aim: To successfully invade Scotland

weather: Favourable, clear skies, strong 20mph wind, good sunset, exposed Full Moon.

what we actually achieved:
Great first evening together, lots of laughter, lots of learning, made it to Scotland and back, plan and locations went well, met the coastguard.

memorable quotes:
Dave: "It's not the water that scares me, it's the quicksand"

memorable moments:
Dom flying around the Solway in his topper, almost taking off, shouting "ye haw"

learning

1. Tide goes out very quickly and for some distance, walked last 300m to Scotland, dragged boats a long way back to England.
2. Throw line makes good boat hauling harnesses, we would have suffered without it.
3. Ground solid where we were, not too soft, however, locals report quicksand is out there somewhere.
4. Despite big flow on the Rivers Eden and Esk, we could ferry glide across without losing too much way.
5. Dom is too modest about his sailing abilities.
6. The Coastguard have to respond to all calls received from the public, regardless of how competent the paddlers/sailors are.
7. Liverpool Coastguard should be called in advance to advise them of future adventures on the high seas.
8. Beer and chips in The Highland Laddie, Glasson of good quality. Friendly to non-locals.

useful kit to have had...
Flares, canoe trolley, bailer for Dom - who used his hands a lot, Huskies to pull boats at low tide, Full Moon Fever flags to plant and mark our achievement, small anchor to moor boats in shallow outgoing water.

potential next activity...
As during school half term, it is suggested that we do something with families and conclude with fire/BBQ on a mountain, beach or somewhere east facing.

Well, what a success that was, other than the fact that we hadn't considered the impact we would have on the natives, and that a well-meaning landlubber from Bowness on Solway would call the coastguard. Apparently, they saw us launch to the east of their house and then having landed in Scotland and seeing that we were then heading well past their house to the west they assumed we were getting swept out into the Irish Sea.

The coastguard scrambled two vehicles in Scotland and one in England. It was their biggest incident in months, and they were so very excited - they almost got their boots muddy. They were slightly disappointed when we landed by the second car, exactly where we intended, and they discovered that we had all the right kit and a half decent plan.

They gave me Liverpool Coastguard's phone number which I still have, saved in my phone address book!

Well, it did the trick, we had successfully launched this Full Moon thing. What other adventures should we aspire to? Who else would rise to the challenge and join our motley crew? Why are we still out howling every month eight years later?

That is a story of friendship, resilience, creativity, adventure and laughter, much laughter.

That is the story this book aims to tell. It has been agreed that names have been kept the same to protect the innocent and highlight the guilty.

Before we head off into tales of monthly moonlit adventures and the folk who share them together, we probably need to think a little about things like our attitude to risk, kit and the weather.

thinking of risk

Most folk who spend time in the outdoors seem to have a healthy attitude to risk. Stock market investors have a Risk Versus Reward equation: low risk and low reward produces little results or break even. High reward and low risk gives profitable trading, a positive reward for your risk but could be dull. High risk and low reward may also give profitable trading but doesn't give a high return on the risk you take. The real magic happens with high risk and high reward and that is where you can see significant return on your investments. Or lose it all of course, see Sirius Minerals for reference...!

The same applies to outdoor adventure. We could spend the rest of this book talking about the three types of fun, the proven benefits of outdoor learning, the quest for adventure, aiming to be top right etc. but Dave has already written that book. Ultimately, let us all agree that arsing about in the great outdoors is fun; we learn a lot about ourselves and others, and the return on investment encourages us to have even more adventures. Years ago, Dave and I decided that adventures in the outdoors needed to be Meaningful, Memorable and Motivational. That certainly applies to our Full Moon nights out.

Let's consider what the professional bodies have to say about risk:

The British Mountaineering Council seem to know a lot about climbing mountains. They "recognise that climbing, hillwalking and mountaineering are activities with a danger of personal injury or death. Participants in these activities should be aware of and accept these risks and be responsible for their own actions and involvement."

British Canoeing are equally knowledgeable about all sorts of watery activity. They state that "canoeing and kayaking are assumed risk water contact sports that may carry attendant risks. Participants should be aware of and accept these risks, and be responsible for their own action and involvement."

On the positive side, according to the Royal Society for the Prevention of Accidents (ROSPA) you are far more likely to be injured playing sports like football and cricket than hill walking or rock climbing. That certainly explains why the vast majority of Howlers don't play football or cricket... or many team sports actually, they are far too risky for us.

We believe that a healthy attitude to risk is to be commended; in his inspirational poem dedicated To Risk, William Arthur Ward concludes that:

".. risks must be taken because the greatest hazard in life is to risk nothing.
The person who risks nothing, does nothing, has nothing, is nothing.
He may avoid suffering and sorrow, but he cannot learn, feel, change, grow or live.
Chained by his servitude he is a slave who has forfeited all freedom.
Only a person who risks is free."

For a slightly different take on risk, when asked "how would you have lived your life differently if you had a chance?" Nadine Stair, an eighty five year old woman from Louisville, Kentucky included these poetic words in her response;

"I would take fewer things seriously. I would take more chances. I would climb more mountains and swim more rivers. I would eat more ice cream and less beans. I would perhaps have more actual troubles, but I'd have fewer imaginary ones."

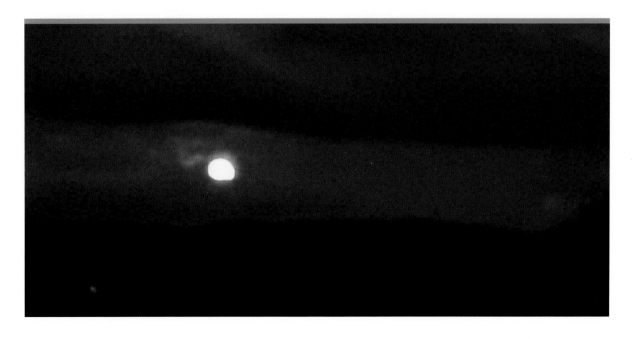

Nadine would undoubtedly have been a great Howler. She could have come with us when we swam up the Upper Derwent to jump off Chinese Bridge in July 2016. She would be pleased to hear that we have never had beans at any of our amazing outdoor Christmas Meals, but then we haven't had any ice cream either. However, in December 2020, three of our ten fireside courses were puddings; Andy's legendary mince pies filled with brandy were followed by Adam's almost legendary tiramisu and then Tim and Kath almost finished us off with chocolate brownies from their reflector oven. I am pleased to report that we still had room for cheese and port though!

So, ultimately, risk is everywhere; in crossing the road, in eating food past its sell by date, in asking a girl out, in not asking a girl out, in buying that last pint of the night, in buying a 1978 MG BGT, in heading out on a Full Moon adventure with us. It is how we prepare for and respond to risk that seems to matter most.

Within the crowd of folk who regularly come out Howling there is a percentage of us who have a range of outdoor qualifications and suitable experience. There are then others who have no formal qualifications but huge amounts of experience. Some activities we do will be new to some of us, but usually someone has a vague idea of what we aim to achieve, how we intend to do it and what kit we might want to take with us. The key is to share that information in advance and have a full dialogue, so everyone is aware of the plan. There are two very memorable Full Moon nights, let's call them "The Night We Lost Andy", and "The Night Where Tim1 Only Had One Job To Do" where a failure to communicate the plan effectively led to different interpretations of the evenings' destination… With entertaining and much discussed results, but surprisingly little risk as both were suitably experienced and adequately prepared and equipped in their own way.

With regards to actual boots on the ground leadership, the debate of "who is in charge tonight?" rumbles on in the background and the current conclusion seems to be that ultimately, we all are. By coming out Howling we take collective responsibility for ourselves and each other. Wonderfully, there are no egos present on our nights out and folk often choose their own level of challenge; on our recent big expedition on the River Tweed, myself and others often portaged weirs and rapids that Andy, Tim and Kath quite happily ran. My priority was for me, Jack and our kit to stay warm and dry; after all, canoeing and swimming are two different Olympic sports.

kitting up for a full moon adventure

There must be more than twenty outdoor shops in Keswick alone. Each will happily sell you a mountain of kit and then specialist online retailers will sell you even more. There is a small amount of kit that you may actually need, and then a warehouse full of kit that you may actually want. There is a difference between the two and it is massive.

Nights out come in all different shapes and sizes but for most adventures what you really need to remember is the adage that "any fool can get wet and cold", so warm clothing, waterproofs, decent socks and footwear, hat and gloves and a small rucksack for your cheese and water will get you a long way towards a successful Howl.

If you want to canoe, you will obviously need access to boats but often friends with boats have more kit than sense and you can borrow stuff off them initially, or you could consider joining a local canoe club or hiring boats from a marina.

If you want to stay out overnight, you don't necessarily need an expensive tent. A half decent sleeping bag, a cheap sleeping mat and a tarp and some string will provide you with a more than adequate shelter and you get the joy of looking out at the moon as well, rather than sleeping in a tent which could be pitched anywhere once you have done the zip up.

The skills and equipment required for safe and enjoyable scrambling, gorge walking, climbing and winter climbing are undoubtedly best explored in full glorious daylight and thus suitable training and kit will have been sourced during that process. We are definitely not encouraging any folk to head out at night and learn new technical skills in the dark. Sometimes just heading out anywhere at night is challenge enough.... Howling is about managing risk and reward, not taking irresponsible risk - it is supposed to be fun after all.

You do not need this amount of kit for a successful night out. But don't tell Wendy...

our wonderful weather

> **❝** Whether the weather be fine, or whether the weather be not, whether the weather be cold or whether the weather be hot, we'll weather the weather, whatever the weather, whether we like it or not ! **❞**

This anonymous tongue twister best seems to sum up our experience of the weather on Full Moon nights.

As the dates for our nights out are set for us by the Lunar Calendar and we circulate the next year's dates in advance so we can try and defend them in our diaries, we always head out on the night of the Full Moon, regardless of the weather. Absolutely, without negotiation or moaning, usually.

Howlers often speak about the better weather regularly experienced the night before the Full Moon when we are finalising our plans and getting our kit ready or the night after when we are reflecting on our glorious success, but changing the date slightly defeats the object of the exercise and unsettles those who have

secured the specific date with work and family many weeks before. I often get a call, text, email or WhatsApp the night before the moon is full to say "have you seen the moon tonight, it's amazing!" Well that is as maybe, but we have disciplined ourselves to head out every Full Moon regardless of the weather, and some of those nights have proved to be the most memorable, for one reason or another…

For our first Howling Christmas Meal in December 2012, we never made it to the summit of Helvellyn, because once Steve1 had been blown off his feet at the saddle before Swirral Edge by 70mph winds, Steve1, Paul and I retired gracefully to gorge ourselves on Christmas leftovers by Red Tarn.

In February 2014 during our snowy night walk into Keppel Cove, we had a measured gust of 62mph and stronger winds which literally blew us back downhill in ankle deep slush all the way into the Ullswater valley where all the pubs were closed due to power cuts. Tim2, Nigel and I then had to drive round to the White Horse at Scales where they had candles lit to welcome us and weren't so dependent on electric cash registers…

By January 2018, we were getting more

experienced at Howling and decided to avoid Storm Eleanor and her 50mph+ wind and rain by heading underground and exploring the Seathwaite Plumbago mine. Tim2, James, Adam, Steve2, Steve3 and I had an exciting evening trying to navigate underground using old hand drawn mine maps. We know where we went in and we think we know where we came out, but what happened in the middle is a bit vague. I later recorded that "the journey back to Keswick was possibly the most risky activity we had undertaken in years! The storm brought down a branch as thick as your thigh which narrowly missed Tim2's van."

In January 2020, Steve3, Tim2 and I actively took our anemometers for a walk up Bowscale Fell and recorded 65mph winds during Storm Ciara. I recorded that "we had little rain and were blessed with frequent lunar sightings of a very bright moon framed by very black clouds. It looked great. To reach the summit shelter it was head down, rely on your walking poles and power

on through. Even named storms don't seem to deter us from having a great night out."

At the end of the day, we live on an island in the Atlantic Ocean which undoubtedly attracts some very exciting weather systems. The last time I checked, attendance at Full Moon evenings still appears to be optional for most, but compulsory for some. Ultimately, we must recall the words of Pliny the Elder as he sailed his ship towards the eruption of Mount Vesuvius in AD79 in the hope of helping his friend Pomponianus "Fortes' inquit 'fortuna iuvat"; translated as "Fortune Favours The Brave". If only Pliny the Elder had survived the subsequent pyroclastic flow, we may then have been able to give more credence to his words. I have tried to check astrological records and there is no firm evidence that the moon was full on that fateful night of 25th August 79AD. I have had the pleasure of watching several volcanoes erupt over the years and sailing a boat towards one has never seemed like a good idea to me… Other than at Stromboli where local fishermen supplement their income taking tourists out at night, and thus you can convince yourself you are supporting the local fishing community, and they wouldn't risk their boats unnecessarily would they?

I think we must surely be coming to the end of this lengthy and rambling introduction. The scene is set, the theatre is ready and I have noticed that we are already straying into the sharing of the odd adventurous anecdote, and some of the heroes of our stories are starting to make an appearance. This begs the question "Who are these intrepid Howlers you reference, and are they all called Steve or Tim?".

the howlers, in their own words...

Over the last eight years, there have been many people who have got involved in The Howling. Some of them were existing Howlers' family or friends who just joined in for the fun of it, like Roger who came for a great swim in Ullswater in June 2016 or the two Amanda's who like to parachute in for a memorable Christmas Meal every now and again. But most Howlers are regulars. From the early days we have attracted a core of random folk who Howl frequently. Some of them even claim to enjoy it.

So special thanks to Dom, James, Dave1, Paul, Steve1, Kate, Jack, Tim1, Matt, Kav, Tim2, Karl, Kath, Nigel, Hilary, Dave2, Andy, Steve2, Adam, Steve3, Scott, Lucy, Richard, Tim3 and all our friends and families who have got involved with so many of our exploits over the years.

The original plan was always to expand the Howling Community outside of our existing social circle. We have actively sought out like minded folk to get involved in the Howling nights out so that we benefit from wider perspectives, deeper conversations and ever stranger ideas of what a Lunarantic might look like. The huge benefits of a widely diverse society are well established. Although the Howlers have

much in common, including a love of caves, lakes, mountains, gin, campfires, mines, beer and rivers, nothing unites us as much as our love of cheese. Links between the Full Moon and cheese are well established across folklore in many different cultures and a survey of American children in 1902 revealed that the majority of them did actually think the moon was made of cheese.

We regularly take our favourite cheeses for a walk or a paddle and our broad diversity is clearly exhibited in the wide variety of cheeses we enjoy. When pushed to identify their favourite cheese, Howlers' answers included Emmental, Baked Camembert, Morbier, Feta, Halloumi, St Augur, President Brie, Blue Stilton, Smoked German cheese and anything Blue and veiny... Clearly we have many varied tastes, but there is obviously room for more cheese lovers to get involved in The Howlings as no one even mentioned Wensleydale. Gromit would be so disappointed in us!

United by our love of fatty dairy products, over years of Howling we have realised that we have a huge amount of other things in common also; very few of us watch any televised sports other than those associated with the outdoors such as cycling, canoeing and skiing, or those associated with beer such as rugby. We are clearly not strong team players as only one of us actively participates in any form of team sport, and guess what that frequent Howler regularly gets his picture in the local paper for excelling at? Yep, canoe polo! Surely this is just another excuse to buy loads of specialist paddling kit!

So, why do the regular Howlers bother to turn up and get involved in these monthly meanderings? In the spirit of the excellent What3Words location app, when asked to describe Full Moon outings in three words, answers included:

Peculiar Alternative Enjoyable

Welcoming Fun Views

Outdoors Varied Brie

Full Moon Madness

Dark Friendly Unpredictable

Fun Mad Awesome

Adventurous Exhilarating Camaraderie

Motivating Achievable Fun

Accessible Friendly Eye-Opening

Fun Entertaining Cracking

Nocturnal Adventurous Friendship

Howling Romp Celebration

Fun Challenging Experience

Luminescent Unpredictable Escapades

Exciting Engaging Memorable

So, clearly common themes of unpredictable, friendly fun in the dark appeals to more folk than you might expect. If you think that you could gather a group of kindred spirits who would enjoy some out of the ordinary nocturnal adventures on a monthly basis then Howling may be just the thing for you! Regular Howlers all agree that our monthly nights out together have a positive impact on our overall physical and mental wellbeing. So, not only do we enjoy ourselves, it might actually be good for us. Who would have thought!!

There is no such thing as a standard Full Moon night out. They are all different for so many reasons, including the location, the weather, the attendees and of course the activity we choose to undertake. Over the last eight years we have enjoyed a wide range of outdoor activities including much canoeing or kayaking on lakes, rivers and the sea; in Winter we have been sledging and ice climbing; in Summer we have swum in lakes and rivers. We have rock climbed, scrambled and ghyll scrambled; we have channelled our inner mole and been underground to explore mines and caves; we have had eight legendary Christmas meals in wonderful locations; we have climbed many mountains and seen many sunsets; we have cycled and flown

kites; we have visited mountain huts, bothys and bivi holes accompanied by a wide variety of cheeses; we have had seven enjoyable family camps encouraging the next generation to get out and Howl; had one hilarious group paddle-boarding experience, danced at one drunken beer festival; had six memorable overnight expeditions and even managed to make two lockdown Full Moons sociable and enjoyable during the Covid crisis. Every night out has been memorable for one reason or another and I have thoroughly enjoyed them all.

scott reflects upon a howling life;

I had walked and camped and tried as best I could to get into the outdoors for many years, then house ownership, marriage and a young family arrived – all wonderful but not necessarily a gateway to the great outdoors.

A good friend first invited us to a Full Moon family camp and we met this group of people who welcomed us without question. They were only interested in enjoying the outdoors and were keen for us to join in. Around the campfire I heard tales of caving, canoeing, climbing and Christmas dinners on a campfire. When asked if I would like to join in, it seemed like a good idea, although that was after a beer or two.

I knew that many of the group were experienced outdoor education specialists with training in all sorts of areas. I can read a map and carry cheese and biscuits but was not sure what I would be able to bring to the group.

Regardless, I was welcomed and helped with some of the more technical stuff, but was allowed to experience everything without pressure, and only expected to push myself to my own limits. There was always an easier way or a route around that difficult obstacle, unless we were taking our boats for a walk!

I find the routine of a date fixed in my diary perfect. I can keep the time free, preventing the usual demands of life stopping me attending. That the day of the week moves is perfect so if there is a diary clash I know it will only be this time, and next time I'll be there.

Being out on the Fells or Lakes late at night when the crowds have gone home is a privileged experience. It requires care and attention but is rewarding when shared with like-minded friends. As the members of the group fluctuate, over time we get fresh ideas and suggestions of new places to explore.

Life gets busy, so it is good to know that once a month there will be an evening when I can head out and share conversation, humour, exploration, fresh air and adventure.

We have identified some common threads that regularly run through our Lunar Antics. There must be a suitable level of **challenge**, appropriate for the attendees and the weather. There must be some level of **uncertainty**, often because it is somewhere that many of us haven't been before, sometimes just the fact that it is dark provides sufficient uncertainty of outcome. We must accept the need for a certain level of **commitment** - we cannot have folk bailing out at various stages of the night, as it would end in chaos. All for one and one for all and all that. Developing our levels of **resilience** has been helpful in maintaining momentum and support. The underlying levels of deep **friendship** we have developed over many years of adventures together has certainly led to very open conversations and sharing of thoughts. There is no such thing as a bad idea...just poorly executed awesome ones.

On most of these entertaining evenings we have actually seen the Full Moon. Sometimes it has been our constant companion, bathing us in glorious moonlight, and on other nights it has made a fleeting appearance to be met with boisterous howls. Sometimes it is fickle and doesn't appear until we are all driving home, and on other nights it is noticeable by its absence and we miss it, remembering it in shared stories of nights when it was able to join us. Sometimes the Full Moon is bigger than usual, or pink, or strawberry or even blue, occasionally it looks like a large digestive biscuit or gets eaten by a serpent shaped cloud. Whatever the moon is up to it enthuses us, motivates us and it makes us Howl in celebration of friendship and life.

Whether there are eleven, twelve, or thirteen Full Moons a year, there are always four seasons to enjoy, and twelve months to plan...

Please remember the aim of the book is to inspire you to explore your own local environment with your own friends. The inclusion of our own Lunar Antics in this book does not suggest they are a good idea or easily replicable. For many of them you just had to be there...

They are grouped together in month by month order for ease of reference and to help you better plan your own seasonal exploits...

It starts in September for no better reason than that is when we started Howling together.

NB. As we often head off on adventurous family holidays when the schools are closed not every month has the same number of recorded Lunarantics. August for example is particularly thin, but we always regroup and share our Summer stories.

september

September marks the beginning of Autumn in the Northern Hemisphere and is thus a month of transition. This is reflected in the weather as you might get the last hurrah of Summer or the first onslaught of the Autumn. Over the years we have had both.

The native Americans call the September Full Moon the Harvest Moon as it is often the Full Moon nearest the Northern Hemispheres Autumn Equinox (22nd or 23rd September) when you harvest the corn, although in some years this is called the Corn Moon as the Harvest Moon can fall in October.

2012 invade scotland across the solway

Eight years after we invaded Scotland, Dom writes:

John recalls the event where he, Dave and I tried to claim the wild lands to the North of the Solway Firth for Queen Elizabeth as the First Full Moon outing. It was a wild evening with plenty of wind, adventure and tide. Dave and John sallied forth on a kayak and I was keen to use wind power to conquer The North. We knew the tide would drag us out to sea, and so had deposited cars in the appropriate car parks to aid our recovery and journey to the pub, post adventure. Having successfully landed in Scotland and claimed it for Her Majesty we realised we need not have bothered as the land we were on was already Crown Property. As we headed back to the safety of English shores, with waiting blue lights flashing, we were delighted with the success of our incursion to foreign lands and the inaugural Full Moon meeting. I, however, seem to recall an earlier evening floating around in the Irish Sea with John, sat on ocean kayaks whilst being buzzed by a seal, we discussed the idea of a group of adventurous friends that got together on a regular occasion. We hummed and hawed, but we agreed that having moon light to illuminate these future epics would be a good idea. Thus, it has proved!

Dave landing in his future homeland and welcoming the Scots to his warm embrace.

Brothers in arms

Dom in action whilst I am only ankle deep

Hail the conquering heroes....

The first of many, many, moons

2013 sit on top paddle from rockcliffe to port carlisle

We have made a point of not repeating our Full Moon nights out because sometimes it is best not to try and recreate a moment which was by its very nature, unique. However, the story of the First Howling had been well told by now and twelve months later the Solway beckoned again. A compact squad of Steve1, Tim2 and myself had studied the tides and thought we would have a pleasant 11km paddle from Rockcliffe to Port Carlisle on an outgoing tide. We had learnt our lessons from a year before and called Liverpool Coastguard to assure them we had suitable knowledge, skills and kit and would check in with them when we got off the water. The Solway empties quickly, like a bathtub, and we lost the river channel in the dark, we ran aground, the water disappeared quickly and we got stranded on a random sand bank which meant we had to take our boats for a walk until we relocated the elusive channel. However, it was clearly the night for losing things. Namely, Tim2's van. We had strategically parked it at the egress, we clearly knew where it was, we had a map and everything.... But it was dark, very dark and even when joined by our friend the moon it didn't really help. The shoreline of the Solway looks quite uniform when you are on the water. I recall a number of discussions about the benefit of tying a glow stick to the front windscreen wiper in future. We were learning so much on these Howling nights out!

It's behind you Steve...

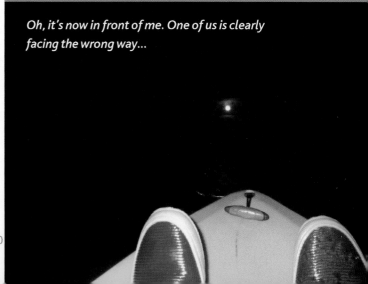

Oh, it's now in front of me. One of us is clearly facing the wrong way...

2014 **windermere swim**

This was a funny night out on so many levels. The next day I wrote **"the whole evening will soon become a thing of Full Moon Legend; Tim1 carbing up with a chip butty in advance, Steve1 eventually turning up, sausages and rhubarb rum, great moon, shooting star, our vaguely vigilant safety boat, the Lake Ranger, cramp, success, beer. Hurrah."**

What more is there to say, other than that almost six years later we do still talk about it. The big learning is that Belle Isle is quite long and what started off as a plan to swim a couple of widths of Windermere turned into a two mile swim. With so many of us living in the North Lakes no one was actually aware of the implications of the mid swim route change... there were a lot of aching Howlers the next day. I blame the sausages and the rum, although it could have been the stunning moon reflecting off a flat calm lake on a night we just did not want to end and at times felt like it never would.

A great moon rising behind the five swimmers

A rare sighting of the safety boat, just after the Lake Ranger had buzzed us...

2015 **ullswater swim**

We tried to convince ourselves that Ullswater would have warmed up over the Summer, so we headed off for a big swim. Four of us started by braving cold water shock and jumping from Glenridding Pier from where we linked together some of the highlights of the southern end of the lake. Having stopped at Cherry Holm, we jumped at Hairy Man's Leap, climbed at Devil's Chimney, ran off the nose of Norfolk Island and then were reunited with our cars and warm kit

at Glencoyne. It was a great 2km swim with lots of entertainment en route. The sky over Sheffield Pike went a most stunning pink and the swimmers were grateful to Andy in the safety canoe, not only for the fortifying spirits on Norfolk Island but for taking great photos and illuminating our way back to the cars in the dark. Having a safety canoe on the water certainly increases confidence on these long open water swims.

Does anyone know how Hairy Man's Leap earnt its name?

Viewing the world from lake level provides a unique perspective on a familiar environment

2016 **greystoke beer festival and bivi**

Kismet is a funny old word. Derived from the Arabic word ismat meaning portion or lot. We use it now to refer to fate, our destiny, your lot in life. So, when the Full Moon fell on the first night of Greystoke Beer Festival and Nigel and Tim2 lived nearby it was clearly kismet. We rose to the occasion; we drank, we danced, we ate, we drank, we sang, we drank, we howled, we drank, we walked, we drank again, then we crawled into our garden bivis, we slept, we awoke, we ate again. The best beer of the night may well have been Coniston Old Man - it is a fine pint after all. The bands were great and the walk home under a glorious full moon would be memorable, if only we could.

On this rare occasion, it appears that drink had been taken.

2018 **hell gill kirkby stephen**

This was all Steve3's idea and a great idea it was too. Hell Gill is a deep slot canyon near the source of the River Eden. It is basically a deeply worn limestone cave where the roof has mainly collapsed to create the canyon. Think of it as a convertible cave. It was well worth heading out into limestone country; the descent had some small jumps and slides, the insitu roped section provided lots of opportunity to climb back up and generally arse about. There were some interesting limestone features and the crawl was at a good water level. It was all very sporting with great fish and chips to round off a cracking night out. We even saw the moon on the drive home.

One small step for Steve3 as he moves past our intrepid film crew.

2019 **river tweed expedition**

We do so enjoy a good overnight expedition and the River Tweed from Peebles to Berwick had been a much discussed option for a weekend trip. Ten of us travelled north on Friday afternoon, sorted the vehicle shuttle with some creative use of many straps and enjoyed fish and chips in Peebles before getting on the water for a few miles before it got dark.

We were joined by Tim3 for his first howl, he recalls....

"An invitation from a friend to join a canoeing trip from Peebles to the sea? How could I resist! I don't think that I realised what a great adventure I was letting myself in for...!

Very happy at home but feeling slightly bogged down at work, juggling a rather too ambitious schedule and needing a reminder of what is really important in life, this opportunity to meet and spend time with this fun, welcoming, grounded and interesting group of howling people to enjoy a great variety of trips into the outdoors came at just the right moment for me. The Tweed? This was an absolutely epic trip for all the right reasons - great September weather, camping spots that arrived just at the right time, two camp fires (with a birthday cake cooked for me in the reflector oven,) enough water to carry us along, some small waves for interest and great views of the moon on my first outing.

76km of paddling on Saturday and 110km in all felt like a cracking achievement and I was still home in time to go to work on Sunday evening.

I was left hungry for more adventures, so pleased to have enjoyed such a warm welcome and great company from the whole group!"

Tim3 and other members of his family have joined us for many howling nights since that great paddle, so we clearly didn't put him off.

Tim and Kath running one of the bigger weirs

Andy in his absolute element, the perfect balance of man, boat and water

A bridge too far? 76km on Saturday was a big ask, made achievable because we only found one riverside pub.

Despite a race to beat the incoming tide, Jack1 was pleased we had time for a second breakfast on Sunday.

The moon joined us for both our riverside bivis

2020 mountain biking in the caldbeck fells

In writing this book I identified that we had only done one Full Moon mountain bike journey, in April 2014. I remember it fondly; great route, great company, long descent, good weather, great moonrise and a nice pint at the end. Subsequently, I was very pleased when another bike ride was suggested. However, tonight's bike ride was a replacement for the planned St Bees paddle which we postponed due to the wet and windy forecast. By the time six of us met at the bottom of Carrock Fell it was blowing a gale with periodic squalls of heavy penetrating rain. The long push up onto High Pike was a development opportunity for at least one of us - the ability of my knees to endure constant pain had declined over the last six years and cycling uphill was not a strong option for me.

I was very pleased when one by one the other Howlers took a hit for the team and in the spirit of camaraderie and friendship got off their bikes to keep me company. It was very considerate of them and I felt the love. The 1,000 foot of height gain was well worth it though, for the wonderful long descent into The Old Crown at Hesket Newmarket where the locals were intrigued to see six wet and muddy Howlers appear in their lovely warm pub on a night you wouldn't send a dog out in. Now I am warm and dry again, I remember it fondly; great route, great company, long descent, terrible weather, no moonrise and a nice pint at the end.

The roman poet Horace would be proud of us; Carpe diem.

At least I wasn't at the back all the way…

october

October used to be the eighth month of the Roman calendar, octo meaning eight. However it was moved back two months when January and February were added to the Julian calendar. So eighth is now tenth, that's not confusing at all is it?!

The native Americans call the October Full Moon the Hunter's Moon as it is the easiest hunting season, unless the Harvest Moon Falls in this month when it's closer to the Autumn Equinox.

2012 grune point family walk and fire

Our second Full Moon outing fell in October half term, so we gathered four families, including our friends The La-Gardes from Buckinghamshire and headed out to the Solway Coast for a walk and evening meal over a fire.

After an entertaining game of rounders on the beach where Dom and Ally's dogs kept running away with the balls and thus ensured everyone got a rounder, we had a great cook out with a stunning pink sunset over Scotland followed by a large Full Moon breaking the eastern horizon.

Gathering wood was easy on this stretch of coast. Luckily, James had his bush saw, at least one axe, and several knives...

The younger members of the party enjoyed trying to howl louder than their elders! The idea of an annual Full Moon family camp was discussed, and this has now become a highlight of the Howling Year.

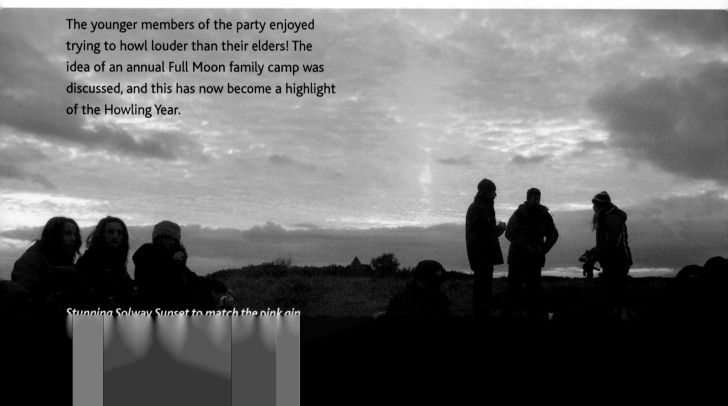

Stunning Solway Sunset to match the pink gin

2013 derwentwater paddle, nigel and hilary's first howl

With so many of us living in the North Lakes, Derwent Water is a well-known playground for many of us and although we had previously had a Full Moon swim here, we hadn't had a howling paddle on it. So, myself, Tim2 and Kath were joined by Nigel and Hilary for their first Howl. Derwentwater didn't let us down, we saw it in all its glory; flat calm, cloudy, sunshine, blue sky, heavy squally downpours, a clap of thunder and eventually a brief lunar sighting - we saw it all.

After a great cook out and evening meal under a tarp, I recall paddling back in the dark navigating by the Lodore Hotel which looked like a luxury liner reflected in the lake. I am delighted to report that Kath, Nigel and Hilary have all been regular Howlers ever since. We should recall what Edgar Guest wrote in his 1915 poem "Faith" "That strangers are friends that we someday may meet." The Howling Community was growing....

Nigel, Kath, Tim2 and Hilary reflected in all their glory

2014 thirlmere paddle

Food has always been a major part of our Howlings. Less so drink because we usually drive home. But food, bring it on. I occasionally wonder whether we are more focused on cheese than adventure. This night added several new layers to the focus on food. We upped our game; after all we were celebrating the bringing in of the harvest and thus we ate like Kings.

Ten of us had a short paddle out to Hawes How Island and enjoyed a long feast that included baked camembert for starters, homemade bread baked over tech projects, the usual array of sausages and burgers and great pancakes for afters. But the standout memory for us all that night on Thirlmere was the rotisserie. Steve1 had excelled himself yet again, amongst a group of gear freaks and kit heads he had somehow acquired a device we were all instantly amazed at and envious of; a battery powered rotisserie, and it actually worked. It had its own special low fire, its batteries worked overtime to rotate the significant weight of meat and veg that Steve1 had skewered on it and he was justifiably happy at having trumped us all, even beating Nigel's homemade camembert roasting tin with a built in temperature gauge. Were we foodies, adventurers, or engineers??

Clearly one thing we weren't was navigators, as we struggled to find the cars again in the pitch-dark Thirlmere night. Will we ever bring some glow sticks?

It was also notable in that it was Steve2's first Howling. He clearly enjoyed it as he has been a regular Howler ever since, but he has yet to produce a battery powered rotisserie from his rucsac....

The grin says it all

And it bloody well worked as well!!

2015 **derwentwater paddle and cook out**

There have been so many "firsts" for the Howling crowd. This gentle paddle to St Herbert's Island for a mass cook out provided us with our first International Howling guests. It must have been half term as Tracy and Dobber had travelled in from Switzerland to stay with Tim and Kath, and their wider clan gathered around them. I recall many hilarious stories around a large fire and Steve1 cooking seabass wrapped in spinach leaves. He is such an outdoor gourmet. It was a surprisingly warm evening, very calm, very dark with limited lunar sightings but we howled with laughter.

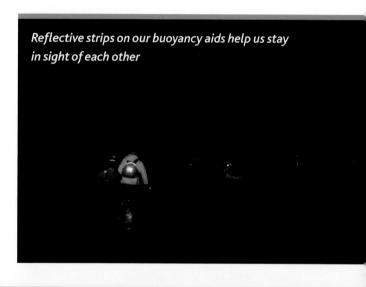

Reflective strips on our buoyancy aids help us stay in sight of each other

A very busy fireplace, note the 2nd fire to vary cooking speeds. It's almost like we know what we are doing.

2016 greg's hut, fireworks on cross fell

We do like a nice bothy and we are slowly ticking off all the local ones. Greg's Hut is north of Cross Fell on the Pennine Way. It is a cracking little hut with a great woodburning stove and a raised sleeping platform. Seven of us took our cheese for a walk to the hut and then summited on Cross Fell in dry but windy conditions. As it was the Pennines, it was a bit muddy underfoot but that didn't dampen our squib, so we still managed to set off fireworks on the summit. Steve1 was joined by his old friend Ross. I have no idea what howling stories Ross is telling as we haven't seen him since, although I think he made it back to the valley safely. "Once is enough, twice is too much and thrice is a poison that can kill a person". I don't see any need to challenge that saying although it is worth reflecting that Nietzsche advises us that "what does not kill me makes me stronger", or is it stranger, it could have been mistranslated from the original German?

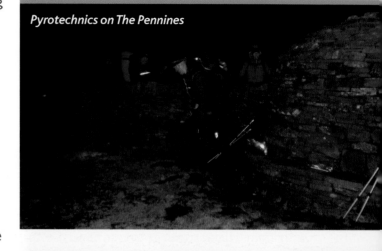

Pyrotechnics on The Pennines

Question; Is there more cheese or more hipflasks in this picture??

2017 base brown scramble

We had a clear evening for this interesting scramble up from Taylor Force to Base Brown summit. We found clean dry holds on good rock. Tim1 wasn't with us so we actually deployed the safety rope to safeguard a traverse along a heathery shelf where a slip would have been embarrassing as well as fatal. We enjoyed muffins, bagels and chocolate eclairs on the summit whilst watching other headtorches moving along the Bleaberry Fell and Helvellyn ridges. If only we could identify the owners of those headtorches, they might like to join us, or perhaps they have their own Howling community already. As Mulder and Scully were so keen to remind us: We are not alone. We descended along the side of Sour Milk Ghyll, logging it in our minds as an ideal venue for a future howl, see June 2019 for further details...

Tim2 and Steve3 contemplating the fact that we are not alone.

Classic old school body belay

2019 cam crag ridge langstrath

It was a wet night as we walked up a damp Langstrath, reminiscing about Dave1's stag weekend lilo descent from Black Moss Pot many years before. We headed steeply uphill and followed the great line of the ridge up to the top. It is a justifiably classic Lakeland scramble and lots of fun was had. At the top of the route the post euphoric fun started... We knew where we were, and we knew where we wanted to be. All we had to do was link the dots together and find the top of Big Stanger Ghyll. The six of us wandered around, vaguely heading north on Rosthwaite Fell. We navigated by maps, apps, the skyline, the lights of Keswick, the moon, more apps, the lie of the land, my vague memory of a previous descent and ultimately the moonlight reflecting off Tarn at Leaves which led us in the right direction. The green-eyed Borrowdale sheep were out in force that night and we saw some frogs as well. They were heading south as we headed north. Could they be a trusted navigational aid?

There are some amazing secret places in The Lakes. They are often best left secret. With good reason, as they are unique, and increased awareness leads to their abuse and desecration. Rant over. We were very pleased to discover that the hidden bivi spot was not that untidy, but it has been on previous occasions. Please respect the beauty we all enjoy.

Suited and booted at the beginning of our night out together

november

In Old English November was called Blotmanad, Blood Month.

The native Americans call the November Full Moon the Beaver Moon as it is the best time to hunt beaver pelts before the rivers freeze.

Perhaps there is a link there. Beavers have only been reintroduced into Scotland in 2009 and England in 2015 because the Old English hunted them to extinction…

2012 **ullswater paddle to silver bay**

With two successful Full Moon evenings under
our belt, we had started to set out our stall
and begun to attract the interest of many folk
who would soon become core members of the
Howling Community. This inaugural nocturnal
canoe journey and cook out on Ullswater will be
remembered by Matt, Paul, Steve1, Tim1, Karl and
myself for several reasons; Firstly the Full Moon
culinary gauntlet was well and truly thrown
down with Paul and Steve cooking mussels in a
Dutch Oven, and Matt providing baked bananas
for us all. Secondly, when we reviewed all the
kit we had taken with us, we realised that our
lack of foresight in not packing a seismograph
meant that we had completely missed the 2.1
magnitude earthquake which hit Patterdale
at 21.37. A local resident told the BBC that "it
sounded like a freight train approaching." We
were all totally oblivious, but it gave us another
story to tell about the night we almost surfed on
the Ullswater tsunami!

A formidable pair of paddlers

*Was our adventurous community
actually a culinary society?*

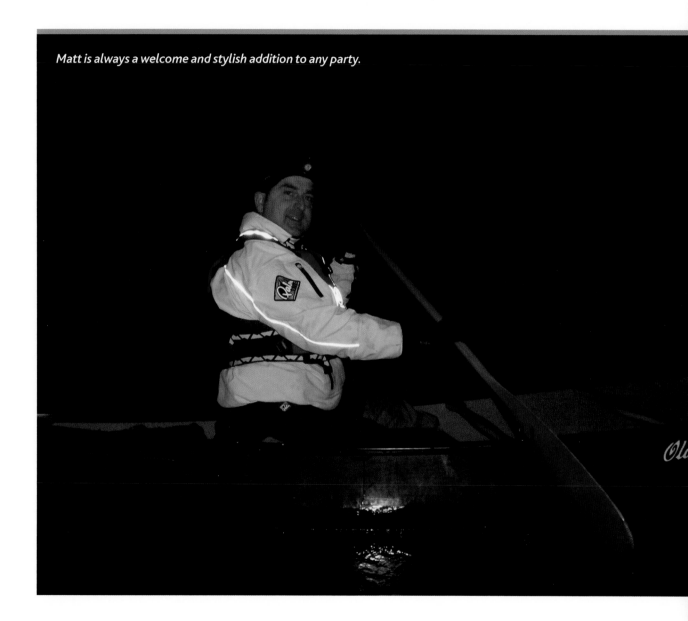

Matt is always a welcome and stylish addition to any party.

2013 smallcleugh mine nenthead

By November 2013 we had had all sorts of Howling adventures; we had paddled, sailed, walked, sledged, climbed, camped, swam, and even flown kites, but we hadn't been underground yet. Was it counterintuitive to have a lunar adventure underground where we wouldn't actually be able to see the moon?? What we needed was a misty night where we would not feel we were missing out on the company of our favourite celestial orb. Sunday 17th November provided just such a night, all we needed was a howler with suitable knowledge and experience. Step forward James - half man, half mole...

My own memories include looking for the Arkenstone, down climbing ore shafts and Tim2 playing harmonica in the Ballroom. I also learnt it is as hard to keep up with James underground as it is on the hill.

seven years later nigel reflects:

Smallcleugh Mine. Well, as you may recall it is one that I have often proposed as a repeat.

It was to me, a fantastic subterranean adventure, something I haven't done before. Being led by James gave me all the confidence and excitement; the worm, the letter box and culminating in the ballroom! What a night we had; a feast in the ballroom, a cavern reportedly used by our mining ancestors to celebrate special occasions with their families carried in on the rail tracks. The trip culminated by experiencing the draught from a collapsed route through to Killhope in Weardale, the other side of the Pennines! Out and welcomed onto the surface to see the moon and the obligatory pint or so at the Shepherds Inn in Langwathby. It is definitely the best howling trip I've been on. Well, those are my memories.

A pre adventure photo to help the mine rescue team confirm group size

We valiantly failed to remake the Olympic rings with glow sticks.

Matt clearly didn't want to scratch his helmet in case it rubbed his name off and made identification harder!

It was glow stick Movember in the Ballroom

51

2014 dominoes in bothy in thirlmere

We have a communal liking of mountain huts, bothies, caves, and bivi holes. They mean that we can eat our cheese in the dry. The weather forecast was not good, and we decided to go for an exploration, to find something new, uncertain of success. Some research had highlighted the existence of a second small hut in the Thirlmere Valley, so we set out to find it. It was not the one that some of us already knew, it was another one. We hatched a plan, headed out in the rain, wandered around, got scared by large wood eating dinosaurs and eventually found a small hut - good roof, dry inside, lovely fireplace, only a tarp for a door.

We had taken dry wood with us (we normally do) and we lit a roaring fire using a blowtorch Steve2 produced (clearly inspired by the previous month's rotisserie.) We ate cheese and played dominoes.

We again proved that communicating the plan is crucial as when we eventually made it to the Kings Head pub we discovered that the keys for the shuttle vehicle were safely locked in the car at the beginning of the night's exploration. I managed to hitch a lift with surprising ease. Upon explaining to the kind driver what we got

up to every Full Moon, he advised me that there was a group of musicians in Kendal that also met every Full Moon to play at the old telephone exchange bothy on Shap Fell. One day we really should go and meet them. I wonder if they have any cheese?

A great fireplace for such a small hut

Blowtorch assisted bushcraft

2015 **xmas meal #4, millican dalton's cave**

With the December Full Moon falling on Boxing Day, we decided to kick start Christmas early by holding our 4th Festive Feast at the end of November. Eight of us headed out to channel the spirit of Borrowdale's self-titled "Professor of Adventure." We found his cave easily enough but it was such a surprisingly warm evening, we actually sat outside and enjoyed lots of lunar sightings. The Arkenstone is not in this cave. Nigel brought battery powered fairy lights and we enjoyed a wonderful fireside feast which included stuffed mushrooms for starters, a five-bird roast dinner with all the trimmings, apple and butterscotch pudding, mulled wine and port. This year there were no mince pies as Andy was not with us. Whilst discussing plans for future howlings we considered a trip to the Tweed. It took us almost four years but we got there eventually (see September 2019) and it was well worth the wait...

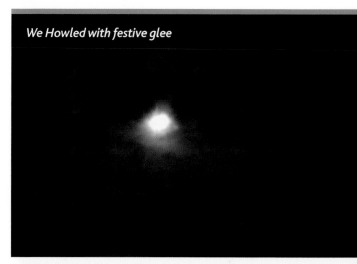

We Howled with festive glee

Guess what has attracted their attention??

2016 **long meg and eden lacy caves**

This Full Moon received lots of advance coverage in the national press as it was a supermoon, and not just any supermoon; the moon was going to be the biggest and brightest it had been for 60 years. So, we decided to channel the spirits of our ancient forefathers and explore the Neolithic sites of the Eden Valley including Long Meg and her Daughters. This Stone Circle was visited by Wordsworth who comments that "next to Stonehenge it is beyond dispute the most notable relic that this or probably any other country contains." Poor old William clearly never made it to Avebury, or Carnac, or the Pyramids. However, we had a lot of fun exploring the stones, trying to count them; there are supposed to be 69, but the number keeps changing...

Our route included other stones and relics, but it is for a minor incident at the less ancient Lacy's Caves that this Full Moon outing is most memorable. We had a member of the Howler Youth with us that night, and having helped us eat our way through a mountain of cheese, including two slabs of St Agur, he felt a little thirsty - the rest is history.

It was a cloudy evening and we only caught one brief sighting of the much publicised Supermoon. We later learnt that Colonel Lacy the Victorian Gent who had the caves carved, clearly did not agree with sweet William, as he tried to blow up Long Meg and her Daughters. The fact that he failed, testifies to the magic of the place and the power of the stones.

Despite their magical powers, Druids clearly need road signs as much as the rest of us

This photo of a special Father/Son moment clearly needs an explanation....

Jack2 recalls;

I still remember my first full moon camp when I was about five because I shared a tent with Jack1.

A few years later I remember being excited to be going out with the big boys for tea in a cave. It was November 2016, and we went to Lacy's Caves. Later that night I was thirsty, so I asked (MY EVIL FATHER) for a drink. I was told I was about to drink hot chocolate but no, it was whisky. Now I actually know what he keeps in his hipflask, but I haven't drunk whisky since!

I am already thinking of setting up my own Full Moon group when I am older...

Long Meg, an impressive monolith

2017 loch ken canoe expedition

Considering it was early November, we were blessed with the weather on this wonderful overnight expedition. We paddled 28km from Ken Bridge in the north down to Tongland Dam. Both days were clear and sunny, and we had a great moonrise and subsequent sunrise with some heavy overnight rain to ensure we paid attention to our bivi skills. En route, we visited both Kenmure and Threave castles and did a litter pick on the island in the loch. I was pleased to christen a three-legged cooking pot I had bought back from an expedition in Swaziland and we had a great veg chilli. Five of us set off originally but Tim2 joined us after he had been kite surfing. We were suitably impressed he found our bivi spot in the dark, but we had left out leading lights to guide him. I remember making a hammock for Tom to sleep in even though he had laughed at my unplanned swim on our last paddle together.

The rising of the moon

Tim1 and Tom, Ian and Andy heading south in glorious conditions

2018 **derwentwater bivi**

This will always be referred to as "The night we lost Andy." Upon reflection, even when it is one of our favourite lakes, it's always best to use a map to confirm where we are going, particularly when the names of islands are often muddled up and Andy is such a speedy paddler. Technically of course, he lost us because we could not keep up with him. We were surprised when he wasn't where we expected to find him but assumed he was doing a victory lap and would turn up soon... What happened next was very odd. We set up our site, started cooking and then when it was apparent Andy was not actually going to appear, we called his name. The response is straight out of a physics textbook... Sound is amplified when it travels over water. The calm water of Derwentwater cooled the air above its surface, this then slowed down the sound waves near the surface. This caused refraction of the sound wave and thus more sound reached Kath and I who had a very clear conversation with Andy. We could hear him but could not see him. We were convinced he was nearby in his canoe; he was in fact over 500m away on a different island. It was quite spooky but led to much hilarity and lots of learning about ensuring everyone has the same map of the world.

To cut a long story he packed up his bivi site and paddled over to join us in time for a great five course meal and moonrise. Tim and Kath's new reflector oven was much admired, as were the freshly baked chocolate brownies we enjoyed. It was surprisingly warm for late November and we all slept well. We vowed not to lose Andy next month as we would miss out on his legendary mince pies!!

The family that plays together...

2019 **cheese festival, shap fells**

As previously mentioned, there are close links between the moon and cheese. The merest mention of a Cheese Festival was enough to encourage Steve and Paul to join us for a night walk. Tim3 was so enthused by the thought of consuming a veritable mountain of cheese that he eventually caught us up after a late finish at work. The evening started well with Paul "parking" his car in a two-foot-deep ditch. This resulted in much hilarity as we pushed and pulled to restore all 4 wheels to their rightful place on the tarmac. We walked into an ideal elevated location with great views west and set up a base camp. We lit a fire to keep us warm; we set up our comfortable chairs and the table that Tim1 had carried in with him. Then, like a scurry of squirrels in autumn, we settled down to bulk up ready for winter. There were more varieties of cheese than there were Howlers to eat it. Six of us valiantly rose to the occasion and ate our way through a broad range of cheeses. There was something for everyone; Smoked Applewood, Gorgonzola, Red Leicester, Emmental, Roquefort, Blue Stilton, Wensleydale, Double Gloucester and a trusty Cheddar. We ate it all whilst putting the world to rights. The dairy farmers of Britain, France, Italy and Switzerland would have been proud of us that night. The range of chutneys was quite fine as well, including a delightful homemade pear. We later waddled back to the cars, quite replete.

A very civilised night out with our wide range of cheeses

The Howlers were outnumbered by the variety of cheeses

december

The winter solstice falls in December. The shortest day of the year in the Northern Hemisphere is either the 20th, 21st, 22nd or 23rd December. Conversely, in the Southern Hemisphere it is the summer solstice, their longest day.

The native Americans call the December Full Moon the Cold Moon as it marks the return of winter.

2012 **xmas meal #1, red tarn**

The Full Moon Christmas meals have now become a much discussed, and much prepared for festive feast. They often attract some of the highest numbers of howling attendees of the year. However, for the first Full Moon Xmas meal there were only three of us foolish enough to leave the warmth of our hearths and homes and head out with our six-course meal aiming to summit on Helvellyn. The wind picked up en route and when all six foot plus of Steve was blown to his knees in the saddle between Catstycam and Helvellyn, we backed off from a slushy Swirral Edge and enjoyed our soup, pork pies with mulled wine, flap jack, mince pies, followed by the obligatory cheese board with Jack Daniels and cigars huddled in the shelter of a rock near Red Tarn. We had to shelter by the rock as Paul and I could not control the small kisu which blew away in 60mph+ winds. We decided that night that kite flying was not a suitable Full Moon activity, or was it? Watch this space.... Despite the challenging weather, we had a great night out and the outdoor Festive Feast became forever secured in our annual howling calendar.

Three wise men, but not a camel in sight

2013 xmas meal #2, lanty's tarn

Keen to build on the success of last year's Festive Feast, we magically acquired the key to Lanty's Tarn Victorian ice house, rigged a caving ladder and eleven of us descended into what looks like a small dungeon for a seven course evening meal. For some long forgotten reason we dressed for dinner as well. There was more food than oxygen in the ice house and we had to finish our meal outside by the tarn to ensure we all made it into 2014. The Arkenstone is not in the icehouse. We set a high culinary benchmark; James bought a hot four bird roast, and Tim2 bought some very acceptable home made port... We had a howling good time.

Howling soon used up the oxygen....

2014 **xmas meal #3 eden lacy caves**

Another Festive Feast to reflect upon a year of Howling adventures. Nine of us headed off into the Eden Valley laden with a steel BBQ pit, chairs, candles, battery powered fairy lights, crackers, party poppers and more food and drink than we could consume. An inspiring location is important for these meals, but the focus is undoubtedly the food. The Arkenstone is not in these caves. In many ways this meal is the culinary highlight of the year and folk like to impress to excess. We started with Tim1's amazing Christmas soup, literally the leftovers from the previous day's work's festive meal, liquidized up and served hot. We then had our own full Christmas meal with pigs in blankets, four bird roast, precooked potatoes carried in in a slow cooker, the inevitable cheese board and Tim2's palatable homemade port followed by After Eight mints. However, the highlight of this and many other Christmas meals since then, are the now legendary mince pies that Andy bulk buys every December. These things are huge, twice the size of a normal shop bought mince pie, and he does the damnedest thing with a hip flask of brandy until the mincemeat is almost swimming. We howled merrily as we walked back along the river.

A festive caveman full of mince pies....

Candle bags were very effective

2015 **family fire and games, st ninian's**

We had already had our main Festive Feast at the end of November, as the Full Moon fell after Christmas Day, so this was a great opportunity for a post-Christmas Family Howl. We had a broad range of ages and had huge fun playing hide and seek and other games around St Ninian's church. We walked in in daylight and spied out the Giant's Cave as a potential bivi site (see April 2017.) I recall us lighting up this lovely ancient church with torches and candles and studying the graves of two 12th century knights. We ate, drank, and made merry. We howled our way back to the parking spot.

A young Daisy planning her escape....

2016 **xmas meal #5 lucy's wood**

Our 5th Full Moon Festive Feast was also our 50th night out howling together. Clearly the pressure was on to find a spectacular location to celebrate our nocturnal meanderings and hatch new plans together. I accidentally found the ideal place. In the Dentist's surgery. It is not often that we identify an unknown bothy, and I certainly didn't expect to find one whilst at the dentist, but find one I did. In an article in an old copy of Cumbria Life, I read a very touching story and reached out to the family concerned. They kindly allowed us to congregate and celebrate at the bothy in Lucy's Wood.

Twelve of us eventually made it to the meal. The meal, for eleven of us, was a spectacular feast, no holds were barred. We had learnt well from the excesses of previous Christmas meals and all the ingredients were there, in the right order; the many enticing starters, the four bird roast with all the trimmings, Tim1's handmade pudding, made with someone else's hands, Andy's massive mince pies topped up with brandy made their annual appearance, Tim2's vintage port, we enjoyed it all. And yet there was still something missing. Well, someone. Steve1 had been running late at work and vowed to catch us up. After nearly two hours of festive fun he still had not appeared. His old buddy Tim1 was getting worried and headed out in search of him. It was all very touching, like a real-life re-enactment of "Two Little Boys" but without the horse. I was so concerned for them both that I even managed to stand up and peek outside the door myself. There was a spectacular moon cresting the gable but no sign of either of them. Now they were both lost... whatever happened out in the moonlit woods that night remains unspoken of, but eventually Heath Ledger and Jake Gyllenhaal appeared together just in time for the cheese course. Commemorative gifts were exchanged, and I received a wonderful handmade yew cheese board to celebrate our fifty nights out and a wolf from an Australian vinery to inspire me to Carry On Howling; now that would be a great movie... We have even considered which actors we would like to play each of us...

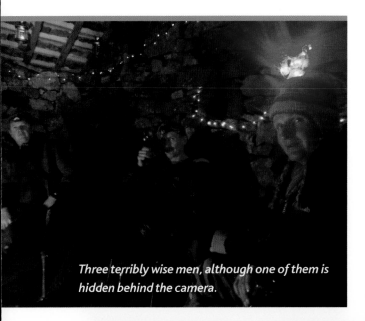

Three terribly wise men, although one of them is hidden behind the camera.

Is Kath rubbing her hands in festive glee, or just trying to keep warm?

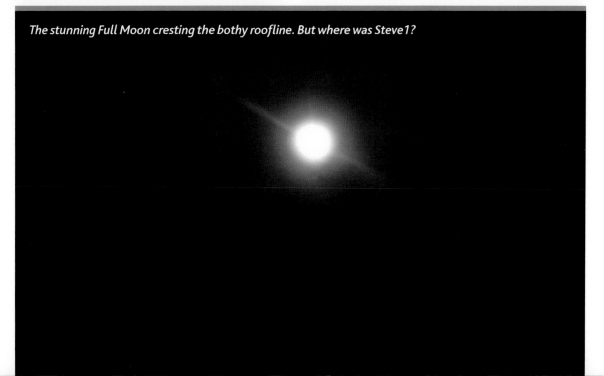

The stunning Full Moon cresting the bothy roofline. But where was Steve1?

2017 **xmas meal #6, rydal water cave**

Rydal Cave was an atmospheric location for our 6th annual Festive Feast. We had clear skies to carry all our kit in and were blessed with great sightings of the moon framed by pine trees. We carried a fire pit in to cook on and it vented well so we did not get smoked out. The candles and fairy lights added to the atmosphere and reflected on the water in the cave. There was no sign of the Arkenstone. The feast was up to our usual standards with a festive soup and a full roast turkey dinner followed by Andy's huge mince pies swimming in brandy. My old friend Amanda made a guest appearance and so did her very welcome bottle of port. We went well prepared for cave dwelling and definitely needed the chairs we carried in, as the floor to the cave has so many wet patches. I am not sure how the troglodytes coped before collapsible chairs were invented, although they probably had bigger issues to concern themselves with, like sabre tooth tigers. This annual feast is always a great start to the festive season.

We could clearly give Blackpool a run for its money

The night's much photographed moon kept drawing us outside to howl

2018 **xmas meal #7 caldbeck fells**

Some Howlers have always had campervans. 2018 saw several more of us invest in vans. It was clearly an age thing. So, we decided that we would channel our inner John Wayne and circle the wagons. We found an ideal location with stunning big sky views East, South and West and as usual we ate like royalty with a seven course festive feast; baked camembert, mushroom soup, the full roast turkey dinner with a wide variety of trimmings, Andy's mince pies were most welcome, Adam's family recipe Tiramisu, many cheeses and some port. It was a cloudy start but the gritters were out which gave us hope. We kept warm around three BBQ pits and sure enough the sky cleared. We had great lunar sightings and we howled, a lot. In the morning, the vans and puddles had iced up and we enjoyed a wonderful sunrise with the moon still visible in the west. It was a great way to wake up on Christmas Eve. We were also blessed with Dave1 driving his sleigh down from the frozen north, but the presents seemed to have got lost en route...

One man and his moon

Eat, drink and be howling

Two wise men looking for a morning star in the East

2019 **xmas meal, #8 eycott hill**

The Festive Feast is a highlight of the howling calendar and thirteen of us gathered for this, our eight Xmas meal together. It was also the night of the general election and there was a high level of associated conversation. The exit polls were reasonably accurate...

The menu for these celebrations just gets better every year. We reflected on the success of our lunar exploits in 2019. In the spirit of the night, Tim1 and I published our adventure manifestos for the year ahead and hit the hustings. Little did we know what was coming our way or I would have included more money for the NHS in my manifesto...

We had four fire pits set up to keep us warm and as we settled down to our ten-course feast, gluttony was high on the menu:

starters:

Salmon crostini, followed by baked camembert, then butternut squash soup and finally a cheese fondue.

main course:

Roast turkey, roasted seasonal vegetables, pigs in blankets, stuffing, homemade cranberry sauce. Not a sprout in sight.

puddings:

Andy's legendary mince pies filled with brandy, Adam's near legendary Tiramisu, Chocolate Brownies fresh from Tim2 and Kath's reflector oven.

Followed by a full range of cheese, biscuits and port.

Three of the ten courses warming up nicely

kate reflects on our festive feasts;

Christmas has always been a time of joy and love in my household growing up. In fact every year it seems to get bigger and more exciting. Since the Full Moon shenanigans began, the festive season can often start in early December... It seems we are blessed that the Moon's presence fluctuates each month.

Reflecting on past Full Moon Christmas dinners, my favourite Xmas children's book springs to mind... I have heard many versions of this poem over the years, one even about an Aussie Xmas, so here goes...

Kate getting cheesy

Andy's legendary mince pies full of brandy are a proper handful.

69

a visit from the full moon

(inspired by 'a visit from st nicholas', more commonly known as 'the night before christmas' by clement clarke moore)

It starts with a whisper of what is to come,
Where merriment echoes the time has sprung,

Be you an explorer, wanderer or feeling a little brave,
December's Full Moon is a date you should save,

For winter comes around every year,
And people from near and far seek the festive cheer,

The Full Moon Folk are stirring and leaving their homes,
Their arrivals are staggered, through the countryside they roam,

All are settled as dusk flies in,
And here it is, the main act rising up from the horizon,

A hearty 'Hurrah!' from the usual bloke,
Followed by howls from the rest of the folk.

As shadows disperse, we look to the moon in glee,
Here come the appetisers, one, two, no… three!

A flurry of passing, sharing, guzzling, laughing,
One of each, more of that, 'wow, what's in this thing?'

A beautiful glow provided by the sky,
As the starters are passed around, no one is shy,

A flurry of proud presentation,
Such a plentiful celebration,

Our tums all rumbled at the thought of some more,
No stopping now, let see what the mains got in store,

Now gravy, now brussels, now five bird roast,
Oh parsnips, oh stuffing, here comes the toast!

To the past Full Moons, we all raise a drink,
To exploring more lakes, mines, peaks, the coast! - KLINK,

For in December we raise a glass, be it beer, wine, lemonade or sherry!
Sharing in glad tidings, feeling blessed and merry,

Now I don't know about you... but I certainly know me,
And I'm not quite full, even after this bountiful tea*,

For I know what was coming thanks to rumours and spies,
A lush tiramisu and giant mince pies...!

We take a deep breath and fill up our plates,
For food is undisputedly better when you're surrounded by mates,

'That must be the last course!' we surely say,
Someone's still gorging, but another's hit the hay,

But wait, is that the cheeseboard? Oh goodness me!
An array of cheeses; camembert, stilton n' brie,

Now as the night it turns darker, the whistle of the wind brings with it, laughter,
For the last course of all, the port, makes us dafter,

Late in the evening there's a somewhat peaceful lull,
Bellies full, hearts full, Moon... Full.

*Northern for evening meal

january

On average, January is the coldest month of the year in most of the Northern Hemisphere.

The native Americans call the January Full Moon the Wolf Moon as the wolf packs howl in hunger. I don't think wolves eat enough cheese.

2013 **sledging in the pennines**

There had been a big thaw in The Lakes and the snow was not suitable for climbing, so we decided that some gentle sledging would be a suitable lunar activity. We needed a good east facing slope that would have retained the snow, so off we went to The Pennines. From the valley we could identify various lines of snow that we could link together to give us a long descent with 600ft of altitude loss, our own version of the Cresta Run. St Moritz could not compare to Warcop that night where we thrilled ourselves with our speed and the amount of airtime we got, particularly on Dave's new body board sledge that no one could keep up with. On the way back we mistakenly drove over the nearby firing range and played hide and seek with the Military Police. At least we did not discover any ordnance whilst sledging. We needed more body armour though; we all ached the next day...

We had been warned. Stay clear of the moors.

MINISTRY OF DEFENCE

WARCOP TRAINING AREA

HILTON TO MOOR HOUSE

THROUGH ROAD

CAUTION

YOU ARE ENTERING A MILITARY FIRING RANGE
PLEASE OBSERVE THE BYELAWS AND ALL
WARNING NOTICES FOR YOUR OWN SAFETY
DO NOT STOP OR LEAVE YOUR VEHICLE AT ANY TIME
AND KEEP TO THE PUBLIC ROAD OR SIGN POSTED
DIVERSION

2014 **canoe sailing, ullswater**

We knew it was going to be wet and windy, so we decided to go sailing. Seven of us rigged a large sail in a Canadian canoe trimaran and headed off from Patterdale in search of the fleshpots of Pooley Bridge, trying to identify some Geocache locations en route. The rain soon stopped, then the wind dropped significantly, and we howled when the moon came to join us, reflecting on an increasingly calm lake. We even had to paddle the last few miles to the pub where it was appropriate to recall the old Naval toast "Fair winds and following seas and long may your big jib draw."

Freshwater sailors are seldom caught between the devil and the deep blue sea.

The Full Moon came out to play

2015 **high pike and lingy hut**

This Full Moon was early in January, so we raided the Christmas leftovers and took our cheese for a walk. It was a cloudy, misty night. We summited on High Pike and then retired in a gentlemanly manner to the always welcoming Lingy Hut for our communal supper. We had the moon with us to start with, but it soon got lost in the drizzle.

However, the lumens still shone through and the night navigation was not too challenging, although I remember struggling to find Red Gate. A very sociable start to the year and plans for future Howlings were laid whilst devouring a few very nice cheeses.

Lots of cheesy grins from a magnificent seven.

2016 **tyne bottom mine**

As is often the case in January in The Lakes, Winter was on hold. It was surprisingly warm and there had been a massive thaw, so this gave us all the excuses we needed to go underground again... Once again it was only James who knew the way around this historic mine, and so off we went on an adventurous journey of exploration. It is a great mine to ratch about in, very safe with some nice flowstone features and small stalactites hanging from the ceiling. We still could not find the Arkenstone though. We didn't see the moon either as the cloud was very low whilst we travelled into The Pennines, but we howled anyway whilst consuming twiglets and Hobgoblin to celebrate my birthday which had been the day before. We only got a little lost on the way out, but all's well that ends well.

Smiles? Or grimaces of fear? James just looks evil, again.

Nigel enjoying a spiritual rebirth

Small stalactites reflecting our torchlight looked magical

2017 **stony cove pike, snowy walk**

Fresh powder snow had covered The Lakes and turned everything a wonderful monochrome and the mountains were calling. We planned car shuttles and seven of us met at the top of Kirkstone Pass and headed east up onto Stony Cove Pike. We were initially blessed with lots of lovely lunar light and navigation was easy. However, the fresh powder had covered everything, including the bogs which were still unfrozen so early in the season. This evening we were blessed with a rare sighting of the McHippo as I successfully wallowed from one patch of snow-covered muddy bog to another, not quite waist deep but close. Oh, how the other Howlers howled. It reminded me of a memorable day on The Cheviot many years before when I ended up nipple deep. We hunkered down under a kisu and had a summit bake off comparing the quality of our various flapjacks and relishing the last sighting of Andy's wonderful mince pies which wouldn't reappear on the menu until next Christmas. The descent to Hartsop was accompanied by some light snowfall which made the drive back up to Kirkstone the riskiest thing we had done in years. This moon was also memorable as it was the first sighting of Steve3, who must have liked it as he has been a regular Howler ever since.

The Moon, Steve3 on his first howl and Tim2 full of flapjack.

steve3 recalls;

Before my first Howling there was a level of trepidation about what this was all about. Would I match up to the Outdoor Ed people with their honed mountain skills?

Then there is the excitement of heading up Kirkstone pass, after work, as the late afternoon light fades and sensible people are retreating into warm houses, in the rain turning to snow, thicker snow… very glad now that we have just had winter tyres fitted. Thick snow at our rendezvous lay-by and introductions - this place is so special to me - sledging and playing in the snow with my brother and sister on weekend day trips with my parents, excitement, cold fingers, thermos flasks, wooden skis with cable bindings. Here I am years later, but the excitement is there just the same. Even when you are older, a parent yourself, you still need to go out and play when there is a knock on the door from your pal down the street to ask if you're allowed out…

Great to be plodding up a snowy path, to Ravens Edge, headtorches coming on,

a chance for me to get to know people amongst a lot of old friends catching up. Up and over to Stony Cove Pike. Suddenly clouds clearing and wow, glimpses of snowy fells in the moonlight, views of five miles or more - almost like daylight. Just magical, and equally appreciated by all.

Well, if the night had ended there I would have been happy, but plans had been well made. We have a vehicle positioned at Hartsop, so that we don't have to retrace our steps and can make a journey with a destination. A stop for food and drink is suggested. "Great" I think, but on the fell-tops the wind is getting up, spindrift blowing - I don't think I'm dressed warmly enough for a stop? Then out from nowhere a kisu group shelter balloons out in the air. I am ushered in and then all seven of us are sheltering behind a wall in a tent framed by our bodies, a warm steamy fugue developing, completely blocking the cold wind as though we had just walked into a room and closed the door.

Food and flasks of coffee are produced and shared, tales spun, flapjacks of different provenance compared with one another and flapjacks of old... That feeling of bonding, that will have been in our bones as humans since humanity gathered around fires for warmth, food and companionship is there. Finally back out in the moonlight, we continue our journey, friendships topped up, new ones started, a jovial team, old stories retold about a rope that was carried but never used, laughter and enjoyment of the moment.

I am quite often a solitary soul, quite happy in my own world, squeezing in runs to get a blast of the outdoors... I think I may have attended over twenty full moons now, all different, all great fun and a way of reconnecting with people who see the beauty in the world on islands, down mines, on fells and scrambles and just sometimes (UK weather permitting) under the magic of moonlight.

Is that a headtorch or the moon?

2018 seathwaite plumbago mines

This trip had been often mooted and much anticipated and we just needed the planetary diaries to align so that James could bring his knowledge to the party. Six of us headed off with detailed mine maps. To this day, I know where we went in and I think I know where we came out but what happened inside remains a mystery. We all thoroughly enjoyed the adventure into the heart of the mountain, but we failed to find the Arkenstone.

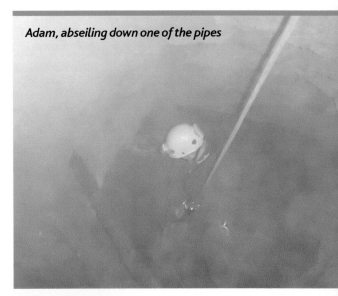
Adam, abseiling down one of the pipes

James in his natural environment

It certainly looked inviting

james recalls the detail;

It was one of those nights where everyone in the county was sheltered safely in their homes, with the curtains firmly shut. Storm Eleanor had arrived, bringing strong winds and heavy rain. We knew she was coming, and I had a plan; Seathwaite plumbago mines, the weather couldn't get us in there!

We had been toying with the idea of this trip for years. I had explored the passages and entrances some years before and always wanted to go back and do the through trip.

Six hearty souls met in Keswick - Tim2, John, Steve3, Adam, Steve2 and myself. Strafed by driving rain and buffeted by winds, Tim2 drove us down the valley in his van, negotiating the abundant puddles. We chuckled to ourselves; what a night to be heading out.

We opened the doors to a wild wet darkness and efficiently kitted up in our assorted interpretations of mine exploration gear and clothing.

We had three SRT rigs between us, at least those three would be able to climb back out to safety if something went wrong…

We went through the farm and across to Newhouse Gill, climbing through dead bracken and jumbles of rocky sections. It was pitch black, the noise of the roaring river below and the gill to our left, coupled with the wind and rain limited the opportunity for conversations and it was uphill. A series of spoil tips protruded from the side of the fell like giant stepping stones, left over from 340 years of mining operations to extract the valuable Wad (Plumbago). The mines ceased to operate in 1891.

The exit of our proposed trip was the lowest of these steps and I rushed off into the hole to check it was clear, much to the surprise of the others. There was a lot of water. It was above knee depth and the great shaft coming down from above was a cascading torrent of water. I couldn't look up and it looked probable that we would not make it through. Tim2 appeared behind me and agreed. I left two green light sticks as markers.

We continued uphill looking for the entrance adit that was hard to recognise in the darkness. Several dead end crawls later, we ended up right by the gill and it ended up every man for himself trying to find a workable entrance.

Bingo! We found something that looked familiar, with evidence of previous passage, leading in and then down! Abseiling was required and we were committed! We were slightly uncertain as to what was below, as the poor mine survey we had printed off was difficult to relate to the passageways we could see in front and below us. Progress into the mountain was exciting and interesting, with the confident members supporting the others. Some scurrying off along passages to try and work out the right way to go, finding collapses and 'blinds', noticing the draught of moving air as we descended lower on a third abseil, each increasing in commitment and drama. "Hmm" I thought, "we don't want to have to climb back out, but at least there are some ropes already in place." After two hours of exploring, we found the top of the 'great shaft.' Seeing the water cascading down, I considered descent for about a minute, then common sense prevailed; we had achieved enough.

We rigged up a hand line to get the team across a rather exposed traverse along a jagged rock wall, showered by falling water from above, with a 150ft vertical shaft below inviting everyone into its blackness. It was impossible to see the light sticks I had left at the bottom. Safely across the traverse, we crawled out through a passageway back out into the storm we had left behind. We had been in a different world, of history and excitement, journeying with an underlying element of danger. The weather was awful, but we were buzzing and recounting our adventure as we descended rapidly back down the mountain. We were wet through from the sweat of crawling and dragging ourselves around in the mine and the rainfall. The rivers below were now raging torrents, and the ground was sodden. We amused ourselves thinking that no other people would possibly be outside tonight as we got back to the van. After efficient de-kitting and with dry clothes on, Tim2 drove us back to Keswick, demonstrating his superb reflexes to avoid a large tree limb that crashed down onto the road just in front of us.

Only Howlers play out in these conditions!

Tim2 and Steve2 studying the map, a practice we all became very familiar with that night.

2018 blue moon kings forest of geltsdale

As we had been so well behaved, we were blessed with a second Full Moon in January 2018, AND it was a Supermoon. As well as being the closest the moon comes to the Earth in its elliptical orbit, it was a super moon as well. We knew the weather in The Lakes was deteriorating so we headed east to the Pennines and wandered into The Kings Forest of Geltsdale. This remote and ill frequented area of upland has no trees and only a few paths as we were to find out on further investigation. We met at the Blue Bell Inn for a cheeky pint and headed off into some initial snow, which was sufficient to coat the landscape and provide us with a wonderful monochrome experience. I had seen the Supermoon cresting the Pennines as I crossed the M6 near Asda and it was huge, but we only had limited viewings during our walk. Having found a large and welcoming shooting box to shelter in, we enjoyed a strong chilli cheese then submitted on Cardunneth Pike and continued north, aiming for a strategically positioned car shuttle. Despite the cloud, the lumens still lit up the landscape and we had many navigational conversations, trying to identify an eerie blue light that was drawing us in...The truth is out there.

An unexpectedly large, dry and unlocked shooting hut provided great cheese eating opportunities.

Adam's Lunar Cycle Clock ensures he regularly gets out Howling

2019 **arctic night on great dun fell**

This was a journey of discovery, and we discovered a lot, including some amazing rime ice formations on the fence wire, caused by moist 40mph winds and arctic temperatures. Winter was here, but not well established enough yet to climb anything. So, we went for a bimble. We headed up into the Pennines and thoroughly explored the ridge around Great Dun Fell and Little Dun Fell which was a windswept icy plateau. We didn't have a single lunar sighting all night, but it was a wild night out in a stunning monochrome environment. Scott had done some research into the local mining practices and we enjoyed learning from him whilst exploring the steep sided hushes. It was one of those nights out where we did not know what to expect and we were very pleased with what we found. It was a great environment to be out in for a few hours, but we were very pleased to make it back to Scott's Range Rover with its heated seats. I

Andy and Scott frosting up despite the brandy and Kendal Mint Cake

remember having every item of spare clothing on and then being pleased to put an empty rucksack on my back for a little extra protection from the wind.

Steve3 had all the right kit for an arctic exploration

2020 **dubs hut bothy night**

Tim1 is a very regular howler. He has attended over half of our 80+ howling nights out. He is also well known as something of a character and often features in memorable stories of our exploits. This night out will go down in Full Moon legend as "The night Tim1 only had one job to do." These words came from his son Tom when I eventually spoke with him the next morning...

As the Full Moon fell over a weekend, we decided that a family bothy trip was in order, so thirteen howlers of all ages met up at Honister to head out to Dubs Hut, which is managed by the Mountain Bothy Association and had recently been refurbished with a new roof, a wonderful stove and some new sleeping platforms. Tim1 was working late but assured us that he and Tom would catch us up, so the main party set off into the wet and windy night, heading straight up the old tramway incline that leads straight to the bothy. The bothy is exactly one mile from the mine at Honister, just a few degrees short of due west up a dismantled tramway that still has some sleepers in place to reassure you that you are following the right historic route...

It was a foul night. We were head-down into the rain and the wind, and everyone dug deep,

Scott is clearly very concerned about Tim1 and Tom.

On this occasion there was room at the inn for Joseph

focused on the anticipated joy of reaching the hut. Despite our waterproofs, we got a bit damp getting to the hut, but we quickly got the stove lit and built up a great fire to warm us all. Well, not quite all of us. We enjoyed candlelit fine dining and good craic whilst the 40mph wind gusted outside. Venturing out to use the alfresco facilities was high adventure enough for us that night. As we sat around the stove catching up and sharing stories, we eventually saw torches outside the window. Surely Tim1 and Tom arriving with emergency cheese supplies... Not. It was five members of Bury Mountaineering Club coming to join us. They were wet, very wet and

STRAVA

Tim1 and Tom carefully avoided the long straight industrial track leading to the hut.

Distance	Elev Gain	Time
3.0 mi	1,283 ft	1h 19m

we made room for them inside. They had also had an interesting night out and had had a sighting. Not a lunar sighting, the moon was noticeable by its absence that night. They had stumbled upon a bedraggled Tim1 and Tom heading back to their car, having failed to find the very obvious mountain hut with smoke billowing out the chimney.

Poor Tim1 - he and Tom had the biggest adventure of us all that night. Their Strava advises us they covered three miles and gained 1,283 feet of height in one hour nineteen minutes. They had certainly been moving, but unfortunately, in the wrong direction. To this day they are the only Howlers to have summited on Fleetwith Pike on a howling night out. One day I must take Tim1 and Tom to Dubs Hut and show them what they missed out on.

Tim1 is a great advocate of the What3Words navigation app. When considering his personal three chosen words for his epic search for Dubs Hut, perhaps "Use A Map", "Don't Give Up" "Going Home Now" or "Only One Job" would be appropriate. Ours would be "Missed You Tim1". We gave the chimney a good clean out before we snuggled into our sleeping bags.

february

As well as having an extra day every four years to keep the calendar year synchronised with the astronomical year, February is a great time to watch the Alpha Centaurids meteor shower, usually visible at the beginning of the month.

The native Americans call the February Full Moon the Snow Moon, as this month receives the heaviest snowfall.

2013 **winter climb coniston**

Snow had returned in all its glory and we had a stunningly clear night winter climbing on the headwall of Low Water. It was a textbook winter Full Moon, everything we had hoped for; cold crisp and clear with good snow and ice conditions. The moon was so bright, it cast our shadows on the icepack and we didn't even need head torches for our ascent. I can still recall Tim1 reciting poetry as he climbed and a snake like cloud creeping up on the moon and trapping it in its mouth; we all agreed it was one of those nights you really didn't want to leave the mountain. Ever. In many ways that night is still with me and has inspired many winter Howlings since.

Summit snacks

The moon shone brightly on the adventurous

This might be our route !

2014 snowy windy walk keppel cove

The Met Office didn't start naming storms until Abigail in November 2015. If they had started earlier, the storm of 12th February 2014 could have been named Skadi, after the Norse Goddess of winter, hunting and skiing. Known as the snowshoe goddess, she rules over mountains, wildernesses, winter, revenge, knowledge, damage, justice and independence.... She was definitely out Howling with us that night. The weather was foul. We knew it was going to be and planned accordingly. Five of us met at Greenside and took our anemometers for a walk. We had a steady 50mph+ headwind as we walked into

Keppel Cove, where we took readings of 62mph but experienced 70mph+ gusts which visibly moved our bodies. The way up the mine track was challenging, two walking poles each, head down and dig deep. The way back was hilarious and equally challenging as the wind was now behind us and was actively pushing us downhill on a path covered with ankle deep slush. When we returned to the valley we found that Glenridding had lost all power and thus the pubs were closed, so was the Royal at Dockray and we had to go all the way to The White Horse at Scales who welcomed us with candles and a warm fire. True grit.

We had an entertaining few minutes considering options for the end of the sentence.....!

DANGER
UNSTABLE STRUCTURE
DO NOT WALK OR

Is that you Nigel?

2015 **kilnshaw chimney red screes**

Winter can be a glorious time in The Lakes, and the Fell Top Assessors' daily reports from Helvellyn certainly help us plan our nights out at this time of the year. At 1.05pm they reported wind speed of 15.5mph, gusting to 32.3mph with a windchill of minus 16.5c. So, it was definitely going to be a double Buffalo night out. A core group of four regular Howlers were joined by our old friend Adam who had recently returned to Cumbria, and we headed off up Kilnshaw Chimney. Snow conditions were good, with some useful neve, the winds were strong, and we recorded our own 34mph gusts on the summit of Red Screes. We enjoyed a nice pint at the Brotherswater Inn on the way home. Adam has howled with us dozens of times since his inauguration on this great night out.

Adam's first howling

A misty Tim1 clearly enjoying himself, despite his very vocal claims...

tim1 recalls;

Just occasionally, the full moon falls on nights when conditions are perfect for a wintry adventure and this was one of them. The snow on this winter's night was old and firm and the route was well climbed, leaving many obvious steps, formed in the icy snow. Equipped with my notorious £2.50 crampons picked up from a charity market stall in the Devon town of Tavistock (they are not well known for winter climbing down there), coupled with 3 season boots and under the bright light of a glowing full moon, our group made great progress up the mountain, stopping only briefly to re-attach my flailing crampon from time to time.

Myself, topping out and my trusty Buffalo frosting up

The feeling of being out in the high mountains on nights like this is incredible. Hard to describe the sense of winning back part of a day so often wasted indoors and recharging the soul ready for the more mundane, daily aspects of life.

Of course, it is not always that perfect situation - some moons fall on grotty evenings, where staying in and feigning an excuse not to go out seems the best option. However, forging on past these moments of weakness are never regretted and the fresh air and camaraderie of adventure is always overwhelmingly positive.

Tim2 in full swing

2016 **blencathra headwall**

Blencathra is such a mountaineer's mountain. It has so much variety to offer and never disappoints. It was half term and many Howling folk were away so Nigel and I headed out to explore the headwall in much better conditions than our last visit (see March 2013.) We followed the beck up from the tarn, and crossed lots of snow bridges as we headed into the snow bowl where there was evidence of recent avalanches in the latest thaw. However, temperatures of -5c had consolidated everything nicely and we enjoyed our finish up the headwall. We had the whole of Blencathra to ourselves this evening. We only saw one fell runner with his torch moving quickly in the distance. We enjoyed hot chocolate and a wee nip of Glayva at the top before descending in our moonlit wonderland. There was no need for our head torches as the moon provided huge clarity of definition between the rock and the snow. It was like a massive spotlight was shining on the mountain. A very memorable night out which Nigel and I often reference as a classic Full Moon night out. Fantastic friendly fun. You have to love Blencathra.

Nigel, well equipped for our memorable ascent

2017 winter ascent brown cove crags and helvellyn

This great winter night out was a big transition for us. We were no longer mountaineers heading out for a nocturnal adventure; we were now a film crew looking for the best angle. I had recently celebrated a big birthday and a kind and generous group of friends had clubbed together to buy me a GoPro so I could record our exploits. The chaos this transition was to cause was at that stage still unknown...

This evening the average howling age plummeted as we were joined by two under 18s and an under 30 year old. It was great to see the younger generation being able to keep up with all the experience on the hill that night. It filled me with hope. Our choice of gully was in great nick, with a mixture of solid water ice and hard neve, and we bombed our way up it. The wind increased as we reached the summit of Helvellyn where we recorded -17.5c windchill, whilst hunkered down in the lee of the cross shelter eating Cadbury's Mini Eggs. Easter was clearly coming and this was likely to be our last Winter howl of the year, so we made the most of it and had another memorable night out. The moon came out to play on our descent as we meandered our way back down to the fleshpots of Thirlmere.

Two generations of Howler

The moon came out to play

93

2019 **tilberthwaite and horse crag deep level**

One of the joys of these howling nights out is that we often end up in corners of the county that many of us are unfamiliar with. Tonight, we ended up somewhere none of us had been before - Horse Crag Deep Mine. We also discovered that if you mention the name of a mine to James, within 24 hours he has researched its history, found the mine plan, and laminated it all. Four of us met at the Three Shires Inn for planning and a pint before heading out to explore a very atmospheric Cathedral Cavern as a bit of a warmup. It was great to have this popular location to ourselves in the dark. It was wet and windy above ground as we wandered south and we were pleased to locate the entrance to the deep mine easily enough. The unfathomable amount of work carried out by Cumbria Amenity Trust Mining History Society in clearing blockages and removing water from the mine is truly inspiring and they gave us a great night out. James's ginger stilton was pretty fine as well. Overall, a very memorable evening underground exploring this 1,000 metre long adit. A true adventure for us all visiting the heart of the mountain. Still no sign of the Arkenstone though.

Deeper and deeper we went, in search of the Arkenstone.

Ladders always entice us to explore deeper…

94

2020 **bowscale fell, storm ciara**

Since the Met Office started naming storms, it has been easier for the media to advise us how bad it is going to be. The increased profile of storms in a country which has always been obsessed by the weather, makes for good reading and provides the newspapers with some spectacular post storm photos, mainly of waves breaking on lighthouses - always a popular front-page filler. The increased awareness of predicted bad weather also enables us Howlers to plan accordingly. On previous big weather events which have coincided with the Full Moon, we have often bravely run away underground. However, this night three experienced old mountain men studied maps and the forecast conditions, and calculated that we could still have a great night out if we planned it correctly. We would be mainly protected in the wind shadow of the Northern Fells, only exposing ourselves briefly on the summit of Bowscale Fell before quickly descending to The Mill Inn in Mungrisdale. We followed the plan, and everything went well, except they closed the pub early that night as the weather was so foul no one else left their homes! In fact, the weather wasn't that bad. It hardly rained and we had great lunar sightings. It was windy, very windy. To reach the welcoming summit shelter, it was hoods up and heads down into steady 50mph headwinds, relying on your walking poles and powering on through. We had lots of fun recording 65mph gusts with our anemometers and the bright moon looked even brighter when framed by the very black storm clouds. It was a very memorable night and it seems that even named storms don't deter us from having a howling good time. It was all very invigorating really.

Three old friends on a night out together, Steve3, The Moon and Tim2

march

In the Northern Hemisphere, the meteorological beginning of Spring starts on the 1st March. However, the astronomical beginning of Spring is not until the equinox on 22nd or 23rd March. So, who knows when Spring has really sprung.

The native Americans call the March Full Moon the Worm Moon as it is when the ground thawed, and the worms started wriggling.

2013 winter climb blencathra

Some of the stories of our nights out get told time and time again. Both amongst ourselves and to a wider audience, anyone that will listen really. What surprises me in looking back on this night, was that there were only four of us involved. It seems a lot more were present in hindsight, but perhaps that is only because so many people have now heard this story. Tim1, Karl and I were joined by Tim2 on his first howling night out, an ascent of Scales Tarn headwall on Blencathra. We were well equipped and ready for all conditions. What we encountered was thigh deep powder with an associated avalanche risk. We picked our way up rocky ribs and welcomed any patch of turf that would take an axe. We weren't really following an obvious line, we were just exploring. Tim1 was at the back with the rope keeping nice and dry in his rucksack. He kept suggesting that we pass the rope forward to Karl at the front. We assumed it was because he hadn't had his evening meal and was feeling weaker than normal. When we reached the summit to register anemometer readings of 45mph and -19.5c wind chill, it turns out that he had been trying to encourage us to rope up. Communication is key.

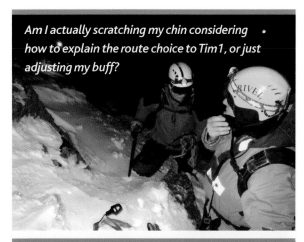

Am I actually scratching my chin considering how to explain the route choice to Tim1, or just adjusting my buff?

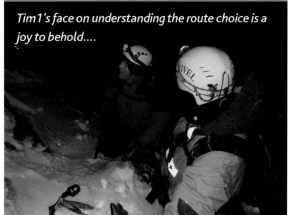

Tim1's face on understanding the route choice is a joy to behold....

Our route may have looked a bit like this. Who knows?

2014 cat ghyll borrowdale

The weather was unpredictable, and unusually for us we did not actually have a plan agreed beforehand. So, five of us met at The Pheasant Inn in Keswick with the scrambling guidebooks and considered our options. The evenings were noticeably lighter, and the previous days had been relatively dry for The Lakes so we settled on a nice scramble up Cat Ghyll and wandered onto the summit of Bleaberry Fell for sunset. This ghyll has great handholds and lots of route choice options. This was our 19th Howling night out and was particularly notable because the community had grown again, as Andy joined us for the first time. He bought a hip flask of brandy, but no mince pies. Yet.

Three points of contact for Me, Andy, Karl, Nigel and Tim2 (behind the camera).

A Buffalo mountain shirt always ensures I have a smile on my face

2015 sledging and skiing on raise

My lasting memory of this Lunarantic is lots of laughter in the darkness as we all shot about the slopes.

Steve2 getting ready to sledge off down the ski slope. If only he could steer

Lunar skiing

tim2 reflects on a great night out

The great thing about Full Moon trips is that you do things that you would not normally do. Even just being in the outdoors at night is a novel experience. It might not be the most extreme or newsworthy event, but it's always worthwhile. A walk up to Raise isn't the most exciting walk, but it was certainly fun on this occasion. I'd made these cut off skis about 25 years ago (before we had kids!) by making a steel crampon style bracket and screwing them onto an old pair of skis. I'd only used them a couple of times, so it was quite exciting to put them on in the dark on a slope I didn't really know. However, they worked! Everyone shot off down the ski slope on their various contraptions. It could have all gone pear shaped at the bottom as Steve2 shot over an edge on his 'spoon'. Amazingly, he'd gone down a snowy ridge between two wind scoops. A foot either way and it could have been a different story. So often the case on these nights out. AOOOOOOOOOOOOOOOW.

2016 **no2 gully helvellyn**

Helvellyn usually holds the last of The Lakes winter snow, well into March and often still present at Easter. The Fell Top Assessors had advised us that snow depth was around 50cm and the summit temperature at midday was -6c, so we were reassured that the walk into Red Tarn would be well worthwhile. No2 Gully is an easy route to find and well suited for a night ascent, assuming you have the correct knowledge, skills, and equipment. The moon was with us for a while, but cloud had descended before we summited. We enjoyed hot drinks on the summit and then came back to the tarn via a snowy Swirral Edge. Karl entertained us with stories of his many exploits, and we were delighted with our last Winter howl of the year. All the bits of the jigsaw came together tonight - it was a cracking evening out.

Karl and Tim2 enjoying well deserved torchlit refreshments on the summit

2017 canoe lower derwent isel to workington

The snow had all melted and the rivers were quite full, so we started early to make the most of the daylight and headed down the Lower Derwent to the sea, paddling west into a blinding sun. We channelled Kirk and Spock and explored strange new worlds - we sought out new life and new civilisations, and we boldly went where no one had been before. We actually paddled off the edge of the map and once past Broughton had a genuine voyage of discovery on a great stretch of the river that none of the five of us had paddled before. I remember doing our bit for the paddling community, as we did some gardening near the castle and cut out a significant strainer from the flow. We enjoyed a warm welcome at The Kingfisher in Cockermouth which still had its handy mooring pole at the bottom of its beer garden. Our 21km journey finished in Workington just as a wonderful clear moon rose through the trees and we howled whilst enjoying sausages and halloumi cooked over a fire.

The sunset provided a stunning finale to a great paddle

A happy Andy with a moon on his head and a sausage sandwich in his hand

2018 derwentwater paddle

This moon fell into the Easter holidays and many Howlers were away, so Andy and I braved strong northerly winds and paddled solo from Kettlewell out to St Herbert's for a slap up meal of sausages, beer and brandy. We have had windier nights out but it was head down and paddle hard. We were rewarded with crepuscular rays at sunset and we sat around the fire pit and watched a great moonrise over Bleaberry Fell. The wind dropped and the moon lit the way for our paddle back and we landed refreshed in many ways. Sometimes, our Lunar Antics don't involve an epic story or a tall tale. Sometimes, they are just relaxing nights out, a break from the norm.

Sometimes things are just black and white

Lunar reflections always enhance a night paddle

102

2019 nab craggs scramble, thirlmere

Six regular Howlers were joined by Richard, out for his first howl. It was a cloudy night with no moon for the walk in, and he voiced his surprise at how easily we located the bottom of a scramble that none of us had climbed before. I think we were all secretly delighted as well but shrugged off our navigational luck. All boded well for a great night out together; the rock was clean and dry, and we even managed to align certain features with the guidebook which is always reassuring! Kate produced a very welcome banana cake at the top of the route to reward us all before we wandered along to the summit of Ullscarf where we did some micro-navigation in the mist and chose our route down to Harrop Tarn. The moon eventually joined us, as did a surprising number of frogs. Some research suggests that amphibians around the world synchronise their mating activity by the full moon. It seems that frogs, newts, and toads all like to mate by moonlight. It is thought this reduces the likelihood of them getting eaten whilst they are distracted by more important matters. Isn't nature grand...

Six happy howlers bridging the ages

2020 silverband mine, great dunfell

The Concise Oxford Dictionary defines the noun 'adventure' as a "daring enterprise; unexpected or exciting incident". I have my own definition which I have refined over many years of being an adventurer; "a journey with an uncertain outcome." Tonight's Howling certainly fell into that category. At the beginning of the evening we weren't really sure what we were going to do. Midway through we weren't sure if we would find what we had set out to find, and by the end of the night we were less than certain if there was anything to find in the first place. But we had a lot of fun searching, exploring, and investigating every shake hole, re-entrant and shadow in the snow-covered landscape.

The weather wasn't great as we headed up into The Pennines to explore a combination of industrial heritage and natural limestone features around the old Silverband Mine. It was a night of micro navigation, landscape interpretation and hope. One of my lasting memories is of Adam jumping up and down at the bottom of the most perfectly formed shake hole to see if the snow was hiding an entrance to the underworld. Silverband mine stopped producing lead over 40 years ago, but there is lots of industrial heritage to explore. On this dark snowy night,

it had a feel of an old American gold rush ghost town, but without the tourists. The buildings are slowly succumbing to vandalism and the harsh Pennine weather. The machinery and pylons are confirming Neil Young's thought that "Rust Never Sleeps" and the obvious mine entrance is blocked and impassable.

Was there another way in? We were uncertain and still are. You could argue that trying to find a hole in the ground in the dark when most of the terrain is covered in snow was a foolish proposition from the start, but find one we did. Moving aside some iron work we found a deep dark slot, just about large enough to descend into. Our powerful torches couldn't reach the bottom, but we could hear running water below us; lots of fast moving running water. We had the right kit with us, and it is always good to practice our SRT skills, but there was a noticeable lack of anything on the desolate fell that we could abseil or belay off. There were four of us out howling that night and Adam was clearly the lightest. Were we seriously considering whether Scott, Steve3 and I could take his weight and lower him into this thin chasm looking for the Arkenstone? We had a lot of fun considering various options but ultimately decided that Falstaff was right and that "discretion is the better part of valour." It was almost as though William Shakespeare was out howling alongside us. All our technical kit stayed in our rucksacks that night.

A happy Scott exhibiting strong evidence that it was the Full Moon even if we did not see it on this occasion

april

Starting off trying to fool us, this month is traditionally associated with rebirth and eggs.

The native Americans call the April Full Moon the Pink Moon, as the wild ground phlox flowers and brings beauty.

2013 river paddle lower derwent isel down to broughton cross

Longer evenings encouraged us onto moving water, The Lower Derwent. Eight of us headed off in seven canoes. It was a glorious night, with clear skies, little wind, and even some spring warmth from the sun. After a couple of hours of paddling we discovered that the Kingfisher pub in Cockermouth has a riverside mooring post, and steps leading into their beer garden from the river. It was decided it would be rude not to support local businesses! In full paddling gear we seemed to surprise the landlady when we arrived through the back door searching our buoyancy aids for enough spare change to get a round in. She clearly wasn't used to canoeists, as upon hearing of our exploits that night she asked, "are you all in the same boat?" We had good craic with a group celebrating a birthday in the pub, which delayed our departure and we paddled the last few miles in the dark, with a stunning moon lighting our way as we howled our way downstream.

Clear skies welcomed us onto the river

Tim2 and the moon

2014 **skiddaw house bike ride**

This was our first Howling that involved bikes and it was great fun. The Lonscale Fell Route from Keswick is a 19.5km circuit with 400m of height gain, and more excitingly 400m of superb height loss. It was a stunning evening with blue skies and a great moon rising over Clough Head. There was a wide range of experience and kit and we learnt that expensive bikes may be better going uphill but they don't go any quicker downhill than my knackered ten year old boneshaker.

I had taken my helmet off to cool down after all the pushing!!

We clearly weren't going to lose Tim2 this evening

2015 **ullswater paddle**

Many of us know Ullswater well and have seen it in all sorts of conditions. It is a fluky lake and the wind is often channelled down the valleys that feed it. Tonight however, it was flat calm. A glorious night for old friends to gather and paddle for a cookout on a beach and a cheeky pint in the back bar of the Howtown Hotel. The reflections were stunning and the moon lit our way back to the vehicles. However, the most memorable part of the evening was when a wedding party went past on the Ullswater Steamer, and the bride got into the Howling spirit by mooning us from the rear deck... We paddled after that steamer for a while but couldn't board the Lady of the Lake.

Adam, James and Matt reflected in the glory of Hallin Fell

James is a professional pyromaniac

2016 **derwent and bassenthwaite lake expedition**

With the Full Moon falling over a weekend, we were long overdue an overnight expedition. Four of us headed off from Kettlewell, paddling solo into a surprisingly strong northerly. It was definitely a sporting paddle to the wind shadow of St Herbert's Island, where Tim1 debated whether we had bitten off more than we could chew and whether to overnight there or whether to stick with the plan and progress down the Middle Derwent onto Bassenthwaite. Faint heart never won fair lady, so we kept heading north and managed to exit the river before dark. Thankfully the wind dropped away quickly, and we enjoyed a calm sunset paddle to our bivi site. We stopped en route to overload the boats with driftwood and found a great spot to make camp. With the tarp up and the fire lit, we thoroughly enjoyed Dave's fondue. We later discovered that Tim1 snores like Smaug the Magnificent. It must have been the cheese.

We have always worked on the theory that any fool can get cold....

A stunningly calm sunrise, looking south down Bassenthwaite

2017 giants cave bivi on the eamont

This was a sneaky mid-week bivi in the Easter Holidays. Four Old Howlers were accompanied by four members of the Howling Youth and we fulfilled a much-discussed option... to overnight in the cave of a giant, or possibly a hermit depending on which website you visit. We planned our expedition meticulously and packed candles and fairy lights alongside our river crossing shoes. I remember carrying in a large pan full of veg chilli and being concerned I was going to end up wearing it. It was a short walk in and most of us crossed the river twice except James who crossed four times, twice with Jack2 on his back. I wasn't feeling that heroic myself and left my own offspring to wade... Adam went in deeper than necessary and Dylan and Fergus followed his lead and subsequently got a bit damper than preferred. It was a very dry cave to overnight in, with a good supply of firewood nearby. We could not spot the Arkenstone in this cave. It is worth noting that the water level doesn't want to be much above adult knee height to ensure a successful crossing as opposed to a swim downstream.

Many rivers to cross... James leading from the front.

Caveman Jack2 emerging from hibernation in his dark pit

2018 **group stand up paddleboard ullswater**

Oh, what a night. How we laughed.

Andy reflects;

Picture this. An eight-man paddleboard being manhandled by five 'howling wolves' of vastly differing heights and weights, all with an almost total lack of ability or previous experience.

As the shortest and lightest, I spent most of my time being propelled into the air, as each time someone heavier moved or dropped, it lifted me into mid-air!

We started off sedately paddle-boarding down Ullswater to Norfolk Island, went round the island through rather choppy waters and then, slightly less sedately, back to the Inn on the Lake for a pint.

Having run the gamut of raised eyebrows in the bar, having all strolled in in our paddling gear, we returned to the board for another go.

We had now mastered the art of standing, or in some cases, kneeling up – not easy when we were all collapsing with laughter most of the time. Tim1 then decided to experiment

with a handstand. Strangely enough the rest of us managed to stay on board and upright, though not necessarily on our feet.

That night, we discovered balancing skills we didn't realise we had, and that alcohol, contrary to popular opinion, improved our sense of balance on a paddleboard. At least that is how we remember it...

Bending the knees seemed to help...

We were laughing so much I don't understand how none of us fell in

Andy looking as nervous as I have ever seen him on a very flat lake

2020 our first lockdown howl, zoom and garden bivi

There is a famous World War One recruitment poster showing a young girl sitting on her father's knee whilst her brother plays with toy soldiers on the floor next to them. She is asking him "Daddy, what did YOU do in the Great War?" When the world was struck with the Covid-19 pandemic, many governments imposed national lockdowns and we entered a period referred to as The Great Pause, we were impelled to stay home. How would the Howling Community respond to that challenge? The answer was obvious really; with firepits, gin, wi-fi, marshmallow toasting forks, wine, laptops, hammocks, phones, beer, bivi kit, Zoom and of course, cheese.

The Howling Families gathered in their gardens, from all parts of the Cumbrian compass they dialled in, the call was answered from Kendal to Brampton, from Penrith to Wigton and all points in between. Scott even managed to join us from the other side of The Pennines. Who knew they had wi-fi in the east? Nine families were represented as we were inducted into the dark art of group communication that is Zoom. The distance did not reduce the banter. Kate ran an entertaining but very low scoring quiz about our previous Full Moon exploits, and we discovered that our different altitudes and lines of sight greatly affected the timings of our first lunar sightings. Subsequently, we all howled separately, not in unison as usual. The hilarity of the night started the day before when Adam and his family were all set up in their garden a full 24 hours before the rest of us. Andy and Sue struggled valiantly with wi-fi connections and we all stared in awe at Tim2, Kath and Lucy's overengineered garden fire pit which included an attractive chimney feature... They will clearly never get that in their canoe.

It was not what we were used to, but it kept us entertained for an evening and brought the community together again. We hoped this was not the new normal.

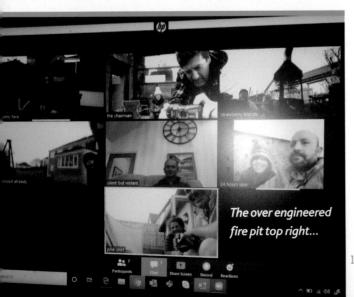

The over engineered fire pit top right...

114

We responded to Covid-19 lockdown with fire pits, wine, hammocks, Zoom, beer and cheese

may

Named after the Greek Goddess Maia whom the Romans associated with fertility.

The native Americans call the May Full Moon the Flower Moon due to the abundant flower growth.

2013 kite flying on beacon hill

This Full Moon fell into Half Term and there weren't many regular Howlers around, so Dave and I rounded up some of the Howling Youth and headed out onto Beacon Hill, South of Appleby. Like many outdoor professionals Dave likes buying kit and he had some very large stunt kites for us to play with. Or try and play with. It was a stunning clear night with a great sunset over The Lakes and an amazing moonrise over the Pennines. We were well rewarded for not much effort. Dave spent a lot of time arranging his kite strings to discover there was so little wind that he would struggle to get it up. Meanwhile, Jack had a very small pocket kite that literally came out of his pocket and flew very well. It was a magical evening of hide and seek amongst the limestone pavements and sunset silhouettes of Jack, Ben, and Harvey on the Queen Victoria Diamond Jubilee Monument. Golden Days.

Dave struggling with wind

Our friend the moon

Creative Human Summit Sculpture

2014 rock climb, castle crag

With the evenings getting longer, four of us headed off to Castle Rock with a wide range of historical climbing racks. The rock was dry, and we enjoyed a variety of routes. I recall great holds on Via Media and a complete lack of protection on the gangway of Gangway Climb. The Moon illuminated our drives home. I noticed that although we were all on the same crag, there was less engaged communication than on a normal howling due to being ropes lengths apart. Ahead of our time, we realised that much of an evening climbing involved being socially distanced from each other...

Tim2 Topping out

2015 **family camp lancaster canal**

Each family camp is different and memorable for a variety of reasons. This one did not let us down. We had opted for a farm campsite that allowed fires near Bolton Le Sands, and we thought we would vary our family paddling by taking to the Lancaster Canal. We headed north from Lancaster and found a very welcoming pub just as the rain came in...

The rain increased and by Saturday night we had a full-on storm brewing. It got so wet and windy we had to batten down the hatches and rig a couple of tarps to shelter under and keep our loved ones dry. At one stage Steve1 and I even had a conversation about whether we needed to evacuate six families to their house, as it was the nearest. However, we decided it was much more fun to hunker down around our tarped over campfire and watch other tents get blown away. Six months later the Met Office started naming storms to aid communication about impending bad weather; I agree that it can certainly be a challenge to communicate when there is a wet tarp flapping in your ear.

We had a number of guests at this family camp including Scott who is now a frequent Howler, driving over the Pennines to join us more months than not.

Traffic building up on the aqueduct

119

I recognise Steve1's feet, Jack1's wellies and Scott's great fire pit

2016 **family camp hadrian's wall**

For our 4th Full Moon Family Camp we headed off to Northumberland to enjoy a weekend of exploring the Tyne and the Roman Wall. With ages of the Howling Youth ranging from four to seventeen, we had long discovered that canoes are a great leveller and something that all can engage with. However, it had been a dry week or two and there was no water in the upper reaches of The Tyne. But we had our boats with us, so we took them for a drive and went downstream into the tidal reaches. There we discovered that

the incoming tide was not such a leveller and thus we went upstream more than down, until we gratefully retired to a lovely riverside pub which we managed to access without getting too muddy... We caught a brief glimpse of Newcastle's famous bridges but clearly the lower Tyne needs more exploration. Channelling our inner Roman is something we enjoy, and we ate in style for two nights at our *epulum* inviting Bacchus to join us for a proper *comissatio*.

Two generations of howlers, messing about on the river

Wendy and Bex clearly channelling their inner Roman; Salutant te qui ad bibere. Those who are about to drink salute you...

2017 **ullswater paddle and cook out**

This was a glorious calm evening paddle at the south end of Ullswater. It was an evening full of food and mirth. After a great cookout near Silver Bay we headed to the Inn on the Lake for a pint. Whilst there we noticed a bridal party having their photos taken by the jetty with the stunning views of Place Fell behind them. Kate later congratulated the bride, only to discover that she was in fact an unmarried model hired for a photoshoot! It is confusing to learn that not every woman in a bridal gown is a bride. We observed an awesome moon rise from the hotel lawn and then had lots of fun watching it rise again and again as we paddled back towards Aira Beck. The angle of Place Fell kept obscuring the moon so we could make it rise and set depending on the direction we paddled in... Small things amuse small minds.

Later that evening our local hedgehog came out for a howl

We are watching the Bride not the moon!!

2018

May's Full Moon clashed with half term and many Howlers were away having adventures elsewhere. However, two intrepid Howling Folk and Masie the dog headed out with no equipment, no map, no cheese and only a packet of mint imperials between them. They braved the fine Summer's evening and the light wind to head out into the Northern Fells. Tim1 must have been influencing the route, as having summited on Bowscale Fell, they then carefully avoided the obvious mine track descent choosing instead the horrendously steep tufty grass straight off the nose into Mungrisdale, stumbling into the Mill Inn where the bar man welcomed them as tourists. They obviously put him straight, explaining they were nothing of the sort. They were Howlers. Shame I was up in Ardnamurchan and missed this night out, I would have brought a nice stilton and a map!

A rare photo of Andy near water rather than on it

An unexpected Howler

2019 **family camp coniston**

This was a very well attended family camp with 46 howlers representing 14 families. When we all got on the water, it was a sight to behold. Nelson only had a few more boats at Trafalgar.
Wise words indeed from the next generation of Howlers. It is always great to see the world through the eyes of a child.

Lulu (age 9) reflects;

Family full moon camping is all about different families getting together and having fun and exploring. What I remember is going to bed late, canoeing and cooking on the open fire. I have learnt how to make a fire and build a canoe raft. We make up new games and play together. I am always excited for new adventures.

"When shall we three meet again…"
Shakespeare enriched the English
language like none other.

Sophie (age 10) reflects;

Every year I have an excited feeling about the Full Moon Family Camp arriving. Canoeing, campfires and playing with my friends are my favourite adventures. One of my best memories was getting all the kids in one canoe, as this gave me a feeling of independence as we got to paddle along Coniston Water almost alone. One of the things I love most is the beautiful landscape when we go on challenging journeys... (sometimes we have to be courageous, like when we go down rivers with waves in our canoes.) It's nice to go somewhere quiet with no other people and just explore. I am already looking forward to the next one.

That harbour is not looking so secret now!

The Howler Youth balancing their catamaran

125

2020 **lockdown family camp, walk and garden camp**

This weekend was diarised as our 7th Full Moon Family Camp. We should all have been in Dumfries and Galloway exploring that lovely corner of Scotland, paddling on the Annan and the Solway, looking back over to our beloved Lake District fells. But we were not. We were still in Covid-19 lockdown. We were allowed out for family exercise but there were definitely no group gatherings allowed. So, a twofold Howling challenge was set. On Thursday night we would all try and get high together by summiting on something within walking distance of our respective homes. Then on Friday we WOULD have our family camp, in our individual gardens and unite on Zoom again. So, we downloaded Zoom onto our phones and headed to the hills, or at least the local hill. Over the next two days, twelve howling families

engaged with each other on Zoom and Whatsapp. It was all very much in the Full Moon spirit. We shared sunset and moonrise across Cumbria and the North East in real time, with lunar sightings for all on Thursday. Tim2, Kath and Lucy got the highest and were rewarded with a glorious pink Full Moon cresting over The Pennines. Steve1 had identified that we could plot our various locations on a WhatsApp map and that made the world seem a slightly smaller place, particularly as some families seemed to have chosen the same summit! The VE Day MasterChef Cook Out was a raging success with the culinary boat well and truly pushed out. We used our firepits to the full and between us produced everything from homemade pizzas, baked eggs, lots of kebabs, piles of meat, baked oranges stuffed with chocolate cake mix and marshmallows of course. The culinary highlight was the reappearance of Steve1's famous battery powered rotisserie, something we hadn't seen since October 2014. It was like welcoming back an old friend.

Many of us slept in our gardens, and later commented on how noisy the dawn chorus was at 4am. It is always great to engage with nature. At least it was not bird flu that we were trying to avoid...

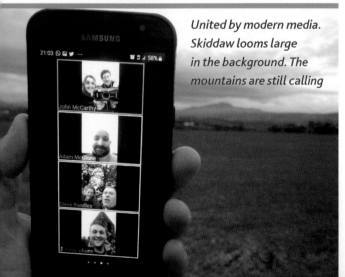

United by modern media. Skiddaw looms large in the background. The mountains are still calling

Lockdown Moonrise over the Northern Fells

Lockdown Solway sunset over Scotland. Wish we were there

june

The Summer Solstice falls in June and thus we are blessed with the longest day and the shortest night. In the UK our thoughts turn to Stonehenge, Glastonbury and Wimbledon, depending on your religion.

The native Americans call the June Full Moon the Strawberry Moon due to the short strawberry harvest season. Picking them by moonlight is supposed to honour the crop.

2013 **family camp buttermere**

Our 10th Full Moon Outing and 1st Family Camp took us to Buttermere in the heart of The Lakes. Nine families were represented and such was the almost magnetic attraction of these Full Moon evenings that Steve 1 interrupted a weekend of work to drive for more than 4 hours to join us all for a wet and windy night sitting under a very large tarp around a smoky campfire. The swim in a cold Crummock Water out to Holme Islands was a highlight, particularly when Ben and Harvey overtook Dom and James in their rush to get to shore. We also learnt that Karl swims like a fish. On the Sunday afternoon at a pudding festival in Keswick, many of us managed to eat six puddings, all in the name of fundraising for Diabetes UK. I kid you not. The irony was not lost on us...

James valiantly guarding the Queens Colours whilst Ben and Harvey show him a clean set of heels

I had recently bought a new waterproof camera and was very pleased with this shot of Karl, the fish

2014 family camp sedbergh

For our 2nd Full Moon Family Camp we headed to the Lune Valley and had a great time messing about on the Rawthey and Lune. We had a short paddle on Friday night, which included some very special American Canoeing Beer that Steve1 had sourced. Thankfully Kate had demonstrated her kayaking skills before the beer flowed...

Then on Saturday, we had a mass family paddle on The Lune and had to negotiate rocks, gravel beds and cows in the river. Matt turned up on his motorbike; Steve1 ended up with a moon on his head; and as we had most of the campsite to ourselves, we howled, a lot, especially when the children eventually got to sleep!

Kate demonstrating some skills on the Rawthey

Two Jacks, a King and a couple of Aces - a winning hand I think

The Moon is strong in this young Jedi

Sophie seems unaware she has a cow on her head

2015 river eden paddle

It had been a bit of a wet few days and the rivers were up, so we headed off to the Eden for a gentle paddle. The rain had accentuated the smell of wild garlic on the banks and there was a proliferation of bird life. We tried to paddle up the Eamont looking for the Giant's Cave but could not get up the first set of rapids. There was a great sunset and the moon was rising as we left the Shepherds Inn... A glorious summer's evening messing about on the river.

Great sandstone cliffs on The Eden

2016 ullswater swim kailpot

The Howling Community has always aspired to be inclusive and we always welcome guests. Many guests have in time become regular Howlers. For other guests one Howl provides them with a lifetime of storytelling. Steve1 has been howling since the early days and had clearly regaled his family with details of our monthly exploits, so it was no surprise that Roger, Steve's Father in law, was keen to join us when the Full Moon coincided with one of his visits north. What Roger wasn't aware of when he turned up on the shore of Ullswater with his wetsuit neatly hanging on a coat hanger, was that we were just about to undertake one of our most physical nights out for a while; a 1.6km swim across the lake to the jumps at Kailpot and back. Five of us swam, Andy and Jack provided canoe cover and James joined us for the jumps in a proper boat. I hope Roger is still dining out on the night he went howling. We miss him and he is always welcome to join us again.

You get quite a bit of airtime at Kailpot

The legend that is Roger and a smiling Steve1 having jumped at Kailpot

Synchronized socially distanced swimming; we were clearly ahead of our time

2017 **family camp abington upper clyde**

It is always good to get the perspective of the next generation.

I recall our 5th Family Camp for slightly different reasons, the weather was so good that Wendy and I went for a celebratory swim at the end of the day. Whilst we were communing with nature, young Tom and Tim1 paddled past us howling with laughter and taking photographs rather than actually trying to rescue their dear friends who had momentarily forgotten that canoeing and swimming are two different Olympic sports. That swim cost me dear. It also helped identify who was within the circle of trust and those who chose to step out of it for a fleeting moment of glory.

Tom aged 9 and Tim aged 40 recall this particular Full Moon Camp for one specific reason;

We met up for a full moon camp and canoe trip at Abingdon in South Scotland. It was an excellent canoe journey; the Clyde had a good level of brown, peaty, dingy water following some rain. The sort of water that it is better to be on, rather than in!

Now to set some context, many friends had all clubbed together to give John a Go-Pro for his recent BIG birthday and he was intent on learning to use it, capturing different camera angles and footage of our daring descent of this grade two river. From time-to-time he would stick the camera to the side of his boat for a duck level shot of the journey. We stopped for a memorable lunch at the ruins of an old castle, before taking to the water once again.

Nearing the end of our quest and with the get out point in sight, John focused once again on his new toy. Not paying attention to his surroundings, or warning his lovely wife in the front of his boat, he allowed the canoe to drift into overhanging trees on the outside of the final river bend.

Much to Wendy's displeasure and before you could say 'Lights-Camera-Action' they were in, taking their first unplanned swim in a river for many a year (neither were dressed for it!)

Following some way behind, Dad and I watched the carnage unfold, calmly slowing down to get our camera ready to record the impromptu mayhem in front of us, before helping to rescue the swamped canoe. By this point we were under the get out bridge and Wendy and John were able to swim to safety.

Now, it's not like John lied to Wendy about how it happened, because he generally just stayed quiet in respect of the damp atmosphere that had clouded the end of their trip. He later quietly confided in his loyal mate Dave that he had been busy setting his camera up for closing shots of the trip when they hit the overhanging trees.

Food and drink followed the activity and it wasn't long before Dave had forgotten the sensitivity of the situation and let loose the reason for the impromptu swim to Wendy and the group. The cost for this, to John, seems to have been a trip for the ladies in the group to a notable spa hotel.

This was the funniest howling we have been on.

Kath and Wendy sailing down a small loch on the Clyde

Tom harnessing the wind

2019 sour milk ghyll scramble borrowdale

There are at least three Sour Milk Ghylls in Cumbria. Buttermere, Borrowdale and Easedale boast one each. Three experienced veteran Howlers headed off to scramble up the Borrowdale ghyll. As its name suggests, it has a lot of waterfalls and regularly looks like someone has spilt a pint of milk down the steep hillside. Our aim was to have as dry an ascent as possible, but we went equipped with waterproofs and old footwear. Someone even snuck on a pair of neoprene socks, just to keep their toes warm! The great thing about scrambling is that there is no obvious set route, and everyone can choose their own line and their own level of challenge. This ghyll was blessed with loads of great holds and some adventurous route choices took us through fantastic waterfall scenery. Steve3 and I cheered Karl on as he put up his hood and explored the way up the final waterfall pitch. We lost sight of him amongst all the white water. It was clearly a night for heroes. We laughed a lot during this great night out together.

The best sport is often to be had close to the waterline

Great handhold for Karl climbing in stunning scenery

2020 **four summit socially distanced walk**

By June 2020 Covid-19 Lockdown was being lifted slightly, and so six of us were able to comply with new Government regulations and meet for a socially distanced walk. The mountains were calling. We planned to join up the seven summits around Derwentwater. That way we hoped we would see the sunset over the Solway and the moonrise over the Helvellyn ridge. It was great to all be out together again with no need for laptops and phones to connect us. We headed off up Walla Crag in fine spirits looking forward to a long night out together. Some of us aspired for sunrise from Catbells, others were not so sure.

The sunset from the top of Walla was nothing short of spectacular, with glorious crepuscular rays piercing the cloud. The Lake District was certainly putting on a show and welcoming us back with open arms. However, the ridge from Walla Crag to Bleaberry Fell, to High Seat and High Tove was still boggy despite the driest May on record and the wind was changing. By the time we reached High Seat we could see a wall of heavy rain racing towards us from the central fells. We donned full waterproofs and continued into the teeth of the gale with windblown rain blowing hard into our faces. It got colder, could it actually hail in June?

Sometimes, less is more and by the time we reached the road at Rosthwaite at midnight, there was a very brief discussion about how wet we all were, before we jumped into some strategically placed get away cars and just like Sir Robin, we bravely ran away. The mountains were no longer calling, our warm beds were.

Glorious sunset but the rain clouds were already gathering

At the start, practising our socially distanced walking

july

This month was named by the Roman Senate in honour of Julius Caesar as it is the month of his birth. Prior to that it was called Quintilis, the fifth month. On average it is the warmest month in the Northern Hemisphere.

The native Americans call the July Full Moon the Buck Moon as deer start to form antlers on their heads.

2013 **derwentwater swim**

The success of the family swim in Crummock Water, combined with the 25c temperatures and warm water encouraged a few of us into Derwent Water for another sunset swim. Supported by Jack1 paddling a safety boat, we decided that we could use the islands as stepping stones, and thus we swam from Friar's Crag to Lord's Island, then onto Rampsholme Island, St Herbert's Island and finally little Otterbield Island before finishing with some spectacular jetty jumping near Hawse End. We did a litter pick of the islands en route which made us feel very virtuous, but also made us despair of folk who don't take their rubbish home with them. To this day, it is still the only Full Moon swim where the water has been so warm that I did not need to use a wetsuit.

Dave2 and myself heading for Causey Pike

Jetty Jumping Jack Flash

Wonderfully welcoming warm water

2015 causey pike walk

It was a warm summer's evening and the mountains were calling. Five of us headed out for a sunset walk, and enjoyed great 360-degree views with the sun lengthening the shadows as it went down behind Grisedale Pike. We lay in the heather and watched the clouds go pink. It was all very romantic! The moon eventually rose over the Dodds as we walked down into the welcoming Coledale Inn. To make the evening even more special, as Tim1 and I were shuttling cars in the dark, a young fawn joined us and ran alongside the car. We all survived, including the fawn.

With Causey Pike on the skyline, we are all looking east. What could have attracted our attention I wonder??

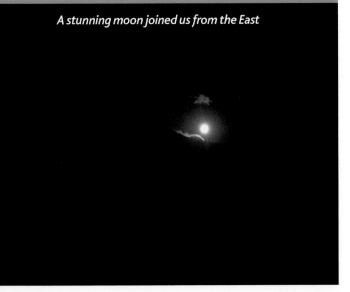

A stunning moon joined us from the East

Glorious Grisedale

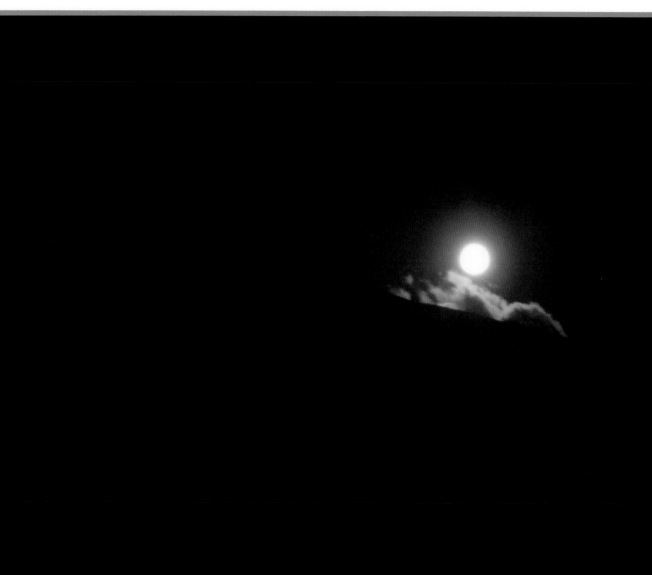

We were bathed in brilliant moonlight

2016 derwentwater and upper derwent swim

Another great Full Moon Swim, against the flow this time.

Adam recalls;

This adventure saw half a dozen Mooners rendezvousing on the side of Derwent Water. We were greeted with blue skies and sunny weather; what a great evening for a swim. Once wetsuits were donned, our intrepid Mooners set off into the lake towards the gnarly Upper Derwent. Having successfully negotiated the death run through the steamer channel, we made it into the mouth of the river.

With the sun reflecting off the Derwent valley, the camaraderie of friends and steady progress found us reaching the well-known Chinese Bridge. This marked the upper point of our journey and provided us with a great opportunity to do our best stuntman impressions as we all had several goes at jumping off the bridge into the crystal-clear waters below.

All too soon it was time to head back down stream. As we viewed the sun setting beautifully over Catbells, we ran into an unexpected but welcome challenge; we met some folk who had just set up a slackline across the river. Ego stepped in and we were obliged to see if any of us could make it fully across. Much merriment was had with many valiant attempts but alas no cigar!

As dusk set in, we made it back to our starting point and reflected on another stunning adventure.

Big leap for Tim2

Steve1 aiming for a big splash

Is it a bird? Is it a plane? No, it's Adam in full flight. Guest appearance by Little Chamonix in the background.

2018 swarth beck abseil ullswater

This was one of those nights that had been much discussed and had been on the Howling agenda for a while. We just needed the bits of the jigsaw to slot together. The weather was warm and sunny. Summer had definitely arrived. We had not had much rain recently and thus the beck was at a good safe level. The pools wouldn't be that deep, but we went well prepared to get wet. We needed James as he knew where the bolts were... Four of us pushed through a steep sweaty walk in. We got kitted up and Chris, who was guesting with us that night, learnt some new skills quickly. The six pitches were all enjoyable for different reasons and sometimes landing in the plunge pool was not optional. As the water wasn't that high, we successfully managed to abseil through the obvious hole. Care should be taken here in bigger water. There was a lot of laughter on this great evening out that definitely benefited from local knowledge and low water. I remember walking off towards a stunning pink sunset.

Steve3 in action

Chris's first abseil. Ever

2019 **himalayan howl, jmc in nepal**

I was leading an expedition in the Annapurna
Sanctuary when we were blessed with this shot
of the clouds parting and the moon coming out
to join us. I really like this photo and was looking
for any excuse to include it in the book! I am
wearing the distinctive Tilley hat.

It is not every month that the Himalayas provide a howling backdrop

2020 **grasmere and rydal water swim**

Whenever two or more Howlers gather in the same place, we often consider ideas for future moons. The idea of swimming the length of Grasmere, then down the Rothay and then the length of Rydal Water, emerging at the Badger Bar had been much discussed over the years. Full of post lockdown energy, nine of us gathered for this much anticipated 2km swim. The weather forecast was not great, but we were going to get wet anyway, weren't we? We planned our night out with Andy agreeing to ride shotgun and provide safety cover in his canoe. We even checked with the Badger Bar that they were open, and we were all looking forward to a rewarding pint, as pubs had just been allowed to reopen the day before our swim. The plan was coming together.

However, the 19th century Prussian military commander Helmuth von Moltke advised us that "no plan of operations reaches with any certainty beyond the first encounter with the enemy's main force." This quote is often abbreviated to "no plan survives first contact with the enemy." In hindsight, the pike head on the shore at our ingress was clearly a warning. This wasn't just another full moon swim; the wind was picking up, bringing squalls of rain and even hail into our faces. The air was also getting noticeably colder. We were getting colder as well. We were well kitted out with some of us in wetsuits, others in drysuits. Some had hats on, others neoprene gloves, some both! The effort of swimming against the wind kept us warm but tired us also. This was more challenging than anticipated. But we persevered and enjoyed surfing on the weir at the end of Grasmere. Descending the river was great fun; initially it was deep enough to float down. Rock gardens were negotiated and some of us walked around the shallows. Steve 1 just played pinball and bounced his way down, whilst others of us jogged along the riverbank to keep warm.

The river soon deepened again, and we all got back in and the current pushed us along to join Rydal Water. The cold air and water were taking their toll physically and mentally, and we had to assure one of the party that toes just don't fall off because they get a bit chilly.

Andy and his canoe have accompanied most of our Full Moon swims, and we are always pleased to have his cheerful company. His dedication to providing us with safety boat cover has always been very reassuring on our long open water swims, but tonight it was invaluable as several folk were feeling the cold badly. Decisions were made and Andy evacuated the mildly hypothermic. The rest of us powered on through, enjoying the environment we were in and providing support and encouragement to each other.

Getting changed into dry clothes was a final big challenge for many of us as our hands were quite cold and struggled to function. The Badger Bar welcomed us with open arms and helped us empty our wallets. We had never deserved a post howling pint so much. Some of us had warm puddings as well. Kate needed a double brandy in her hot chocolate to try and help her toes thaw out... The Pike Head should have warned us that there was trouble ahead. But we all survived, and after a few telling's of the tale, we clearly had been swimming through sheets of pack ice. At least that is how I choose to remember it.

Rain or hail bouncing off Grasmere

James inflated his dry suit and floated most of the way...

august

If Julius Caesar can have a month named after him, so can his adopted son Augustus. He was the first Roman Emperor and they could have whatever they like, could they not? He did conquer Egypt after all.

The native Americans call the August Full Moon the Sturgeon Moon, as it is the easiest month to catch these big fish in the Great Lakes.

Because August is prime school holiday time, we have had very few Lunarantic adventures in this month as we are often away Howling with our families elsewhere.

2013 sea kayak ullswater

On another gloriously calm night, four of us paddled sea kayaks the length of Ullswater, from Patterdale to Pooley Bridge. The lake was so flat we covered the eight miles in record time and had time for a pint before the Full Moon crested over Place Fell. This core grouping of Steve1, Tim1, Tim2 and myself have howled together many times since this paddle, but I can still remember the funny stories we shared that night, of our various Summer Trips including Steve1 telling us of hailstones the size of golf balls which trashed his tent in France and Tim1 delighting us with stories of how he saved money on accommodation by spending more on kit. Perhaps there was something in the air that night that made us laugh our way down the lake, or perhaps we just hadn't seen much of each other over the summer...

Tim1 practising his howl before the moon had even risen...

2014 kite flying, hadrian's wall

Lots of Howling folk were away on Summer holidays so the elite of the previous years' kite flying squad dodged the rain in The Lakes and headed up to the heights of Hadrian's Wall and actually found some wind on this occasion. We missed Dave1 and his big wings though. He would have been able to get them off the floor this time...

Dom is clearly framed as a rose between two thorns.

2016 **river eden paddle, carlisle to rockcliffe**

Lots of the regular Howlers were on their travels so Steve2 and I were joined by family friend David who was en route to Scotland with his family. We had a great three men in a boat experience paddling the Eden from Carlisle to Rockcliffe. This little paddled stretch of the river was very rural, had great wildlife, had a surprisingly low level of rubbish and as it headed mainly westward, we had a glorious paddle towards the setting sun. A relaxing summer's evening paddle with a welcome pub at the end. The moon rose to join us on our drive home.

Smiles abound as we channel the spirit of Jerome K. Jerome

practical advice and guidance

This book was conceived to inform, to inspire, and to enthuse. It also celebrates our successes and failures, and records our learning. It was clearly never meant as a guidebook telling you what kit to take and where to park. I encourage you to do your own research into your own local environment, whether you live in Lockerbie, The Lakes, Liverpool or London. Studying guidebooks and maps looking for inspiration is all part of the fun leading up to a great night out. Locate high ground facing east and take your camera and binoculars. Do not change the dates to run away from bad weather; it can be spectacular, although sometimes it is just wet.

Once you have gathered a few folk who want to howl with you, share your ideas, decide on one thing that suits you all and then make some decisions about time, place and kit.

You will need to agree a suitable level of **challenge**, accept that any night out will have an inherent level of **uncertainty**, motivate yourselves to ensure total **commitment**, recognise the need to develop **resilience**, as things don't always go as planned but by developing a strong **friendship** you will become less concerned about failure as it's just another opportunity for learning, and another story to tell and another Howling joke to laugh at.

During the Howling, leave your egos behind and your work at work. Let the evening take over, live for the moment, notice which direction the frogs are moving in, feast on cheese, laugh a lot and howl vigorously whenever the moon joins you.

After your night out, share some photos, record your memories and reflections, then share with a wider group along with the dates of the next few Full Moons. In my experience, the right sort of people will be attracted to join you if your exploits are worthy. Afterall, people like people like themselves. If you can't attract the right sort of people straight away, you might want to advertise for folk called Steve or Tim as they always seem to be up for an adventure... But NEVER place an advert for anyone called Dom.

future lunarantics

None of us can tell what the future holds. When we first discussed the whole Full Moon thing, we had no idea if it had legs and we probably only started taking it seriously once we had a dozen or so folk receiving the monthly email. It has gathered a momentum all of its own and we still occasionally bump into new Howlers who want to join us. Tim3 and his family are our latest additions and it is great to have some fresh blood onboard.

As I write this paragraph, there is a growing pile of hats, gloves, waterproofs, maps, head torches and cameras by my back door. Tonight is a Full Moon and six of us are heading out on what we anticipate will be a wet mountain bike ride in the Northern Fells. The anticipation has been growing for days as the emails circulated, and we swapped ideas of what to do. Earlier this week, we discarded the original long discussed idea of a sea kayak trip around St Bees Head due to the forecasted heavy rain and winds. We considered a wet gorge scramble but were concerned about possible rising water levels. We settled on a mountain bike journey as it will keep us warm even if we are wet. We have carried out the necessary Covid related risk assessments and

ensured that The Crown at Hesket Newmarket is open tonight. It will be another great night out; they always are.

In the course of planning tonight's Lunarantic, we have also identified three or four other ideas we can consider for our future nights out together. Tonight will be my 84th Full Moon Adventure in the UK. Between the six of us heading out into the wild weather we will have collectively attended 247 Howlings together. We will discuss future adventures tonight; we are bound to. This Full Moon thing has proved itself worthy of the ongoing commitment. The fun, the adventures, the camaraderie, and the laughter have made it all worthwhile.

NASA are currently progressing their Artemis Programme and plan to have the first woman and the next man on the moon in 2024. They aim to permanently establish a lunar base as a stepping stone to further exploration of Mars. Artemis is the Greek Goddess of the moon, the daughter of Zeus and Leto, and twin sister to Apollo. I have checked their astronaut recruitment website and none of the current Howlers meet the stringent NASA requirements, but we will follow the development of the Artemis programme with interest. Anyway, it takes three days to get to The Moon so the launch would have to fit into a Bank Holiday weekend. Perhaps one of our Howler

Youth might rise to the future challenge. They have all been well trained and would be a great asset to any lunar mission.

reflections

My life has been full of ideas and I will readily admit they haven't all been good ones; trying to swim round to join the cliff divers in Acapulco just because Elvis had, wasn't one of my finer moments, and Andy and I have vowed never to drink Mezcal together again. However, this whole Full Moon thing has proved to have been one of the better ideas. Uniting for an adventurous evening once a month is enough to form a community. Even if not everyone can always join us, they can still read all about it, share the jokes, enjoy the photos and watch the videos. In days when most of us communicate remotely, it is increasingly important to find excuses to meet up and enjoy each other's company in person. The interaction of the human spirit is an integral part of our humanity. Rise to the challenge, seek the opportunity, gather the clans, and get out Howling. You might even enjoy it. Eventually.

Asking Wendy to marry me was probably the best idea though. Ever.

My life has also been full of music. Great

Music. Pink Floyd's classic album Dark Side of The Moon, is not actually about the moon at all. Side 1 explores the details of living a life unfulfilled. Side 2 explores the root causes of the unfulfilled life. It consistently challenges perceptions and provides much food for thought… "Money, so they say, is the root of all evil today.." may be as true now as it was in 1973 but I thank you for investing your hard earned cash in this book. I hope you feel it was well spent and you get a good return on the investment.

Our Moon is a global superstar (although not an actual star of course.) It is shared by us, it unites us and inspires us. Artists, musicians, and cinematographers all draw upon the moon as a point of reference. In Thailand, since 1985, thousands of partygoers celebrate with the moon each month. In Cumbria, a handful of seasoned adventurers go out to howl with it.

Thankfully, no one owns the moon. On 27th January 1967 it was agreed by 109 nations who signed the Outer Space Treaty that no matter whose national flags are planted on the moon; no nation can own it. In effect that means we all own it, so I think it is our duty to go out and make the best of the opportunities that ownership provides... Let our moon light up your life.

We did not set out to write a book. It started being discussed around the time we had had fifty nights out together. There seemed no going back from the Howling by then, as we had become part of a broad Fellowship. I am sure that we will carry on with our strange and unpredictable nights out, as it seems to be keeping us all young at heart. I hope the book inspires some other folk to get out Howling. We will be keeping an ear open for you...

I would like to end this rambling tale with some profound and relevant thoughts from the Grateful Dead, who provided the soundtrack to my hitch hiking adventures across the USA in 1987;

"Sometimes the light's all shinin' on me,
Other times I can barely see
Lately it occurs to me
What a long strange trip it's been"

Happy Trails from The Fellowship of The Moon,
Who still haven't found the bloody Arkenstone.

further reading for lakeland adventurers

There are so many great books out there to help you consider options and plan your own Lunarantics. Here are some of my favourites. They are well thumbed and much used.

Collins Guide to the Night Sky

All eight Pictorial Guides to The Lakeland Fells *by A. Wainwright*

Lake District Winter Climbs *by Brian Davison*

Swimhiking in the Lake District and North East England *by Peter Hayes*

White Water Lake District *by Stuart Miller*

Scottish Canoe Touring *edited by Eddie Palmer*

Beneath the Lakeland Fells *by the Cumbria Amenity Trust Mining History Society*

Scrambles in the Lake District *by R.B. Evans*

More Scrambles in the Lake District *by R.B.Evans*

1;25,000 Ordnance Survey Maps

author's acknowledgements

John would like to pass on his love and thanks to
all Howlers great and small.
Your years of enthusiasm and your inspired
suggestions for our wonderful nights out has
kept the wind in our sails and our eyes focused
on the horizon. I am always looking forward to
whatever random chaos we concoct for the next
month's Howl.

Special thanks to Anna Richards for taking my
scribblings and turning them into a book.
Special thanks to Jane Moffett for her ongoing
support, feedback and guidance.

There have been so many people who have
directly or indirectly supported the concept
of this book by sharing photos and providing
feedback, special thanks to you all, you know
who you are.

happy trails

LUNARANTICS